How to write readable English

Simple English is no one's mother tongue. It has to be worked for.

> . . . Jacques Barzun, as quoted in *The Editorial Eye*,
> May 1980.

How to write readable English

George R. Klare

Hutchinson
London Melbourne Sydney Auckland Johannesburg

Hutchinson & Co. (Publishers) Ltd

An imprint of the Hutchinson Publishing Group

17–21 Conway Street, London W1P 6JD

Hutchinson Publishing Group (Australia) Pty Ltd
16–22 Church Street, Hawthorn, Melbourne, Victoria 3122

Hutchinson Group (NZ) Ltd
32–34 View Road, PO Box 40-086, Glenfield, Auckland 10

Hutchinson Group (SA) (Pty) Ltd
PO Box 337, Bergvlei 2012, South Africa

Fourth edition published by REM Co. Inc., USA 1980 as
A Manual for Readable Writing

Fifth edition published by Hutchinson 1985

Typeset in VIP Meridien by
D. P. Media Limited, Hitchin, Hertfordshire

Printed and bound in Great Britain by
Anchor Brendon Ltd, Tiptree, Essex

British Library Cataloguing in Publication Data

Klare, George R.
  How to write readable English.—5th ed.
  1. English language—Rhetoric
  I. Title   II. Klare, George. A manual for
  readable writing
  808'.042   PE1408

Library of Congress Catalog Card Number

Fourth revised edition 75–7506

ISBN 0 09 159611 4

Contents

Foreword
by Colin Harrison

Whenever specialists in the reading field offer courses or workshops on how to produce readable writing, the same thing happens. Scores of people apply. The reason for this is simple – the number of people whose job in- cludes writing for a wide audience is enormous. Journal- ists and text-book authors are by no means the only people who need to be able to write clearly and well. Thousands of others, including people in the social ser- vices, the armed forces, the health care field, marketing and industry are authors too. They have to write letters, booklets, reports, leaflets, summaries and instructions for other people to read. Very often, the potential audience for their writing is the ordinary person, a non-specialist in their subject, and quite possibly someone whose vocabulary, reading skills and motivation to read are below average.

The many thousands of authors of this type of material generally have two things in common – they are special- ists in their field, and they are not specialists in writing. If you are such an author, take heart. The fact that you have picked up this book suggests that you have already real- ized two important facts, namely that (a) specialists in areas other than writing are often very poor at communicating with a general audience, and (b) there is plenty of assistance available if you wish to seek it.

One problem, however, which faces anyone who wishes to seek advice on how to improve their writing is the sheer volume of research which has been done on the subject. If we consider studies in reading research alone we are faced with the problem that the number of these published trebled in the decade 1960–70, and trebled *again* in the decade 1970–80. Fortunately for us, George Klare has been in the forefront of reading research for thirty years, and is widely regarded as the leading scholar in the world in the special field of readability. In 1981, he received the Oscar S. Causey Award, which is given by reading researchers to the person they regard as having contributed outstanding scholarship and service to the reading field. One other great gift which George possesses is that of being able to write lucidly on the most difficult subjects, and it will be no surprise to me if this book becomes a standard reference for students of reading research, as well as for authors, since it contains so much which will be of value to both groups.

The handbook presents, in a clearly-organized setting, the fruits of George Klare's own research into producing readable prose, together with a careful and authoritative account of the results of hundreds of other research studies. The suggestions and recommendations are based on research, not intuition. This edition of the handbook has also benefited from revisions to take account of recent research into text structure and writing processes. The careful editorial work of Judy Klare has also contributed to making it a source of reference which will be of great value to authors, researchers and teachers alike.

Nottingham, 1985

About the Author

George R. Klare, BA cum laude, 1946, MA, 1947, PhD, 1950, University of Minnesota, is now Distinguished Professor in the Psychology Department at Ohio University in Athens, Ohio. He has wide experience in teaching, administration, and research. His interests include many contributions in the fields of readability, communication and education as a consultant, writer, editor and speaker. He is listed in *Who's Who in the World*, *Who's Who in America*, and *American Men and Women of Science*. His publications are many over the past thirty years in the field of readability, reading, technical writing, and the psychology of language and communication. His book, *The Measurement of Readability*, Iowa State University Press, 1963, is a standard reference.

About the Editor

Judy Klare holds an MA degree in psychology from the University of Minnesota. She has had teaching experience at the junior high, community college, and university levels, and also directed the Study Skills programme at the Student Development Center at Ohio University for several years. Most recently, she served as editor at the Mid-America Center for Bilingual Materials Development, the University of Iowa. With her husband, she currently acts as an instructor and editorial consultant on readable writing. She is a member of the Society for Technical Communication, and a registered psychologist in the State of Ohio.

Fifth Revised Edition

An Overview

Consider using this overview as:

- a preview of organization and content before reading the handbook, and
- a review and reminder of major points after reading the handbook.

The statements will in most cases probably be meaningful as presented. If you want more detail about any point before going on, however, the chapter designations will help you know where to turn in the body of the handbook to find added information easily.

In this fifth revision of *How to Write Readable English*, the chapters proceed from discussion of the reading process to the writing process. Chapters on important reader characteristics precede chapters on outlining and organizing and on writing and rewriting. The final chapter describes ways of judging readability for intended readers. Summaries of each of the chapters now follow.

From Chapter 1, Introduction

Writing to inform or instruct has been growing more difficult because of two major trends:

- Reading demands have increased; and
- Reading skills have not kept pace.

One way to handle today's growing problem is to try to make writing more readable. This problem has two quite different aspects: **predicting** how readable a piece of writing will be to a reader, and **producing** a piece of writing that a reader will find readable.

Prediction can be relatively simple when done statistically with so-called 'readability formulas'. These formulas, though far from perfectly accurate, can usually do a much better job than a human judge of writing.

Production is far more complex. It involves careful organization (typically preceded by outlining for lengthy material), cohesive (coherent) sentences, familiar words, and clear sentence structures. The handbook emphasizes **suggestions** that can make informative or instructional writing more readable.

The ensuing six chapters add details to a simple model presented at the end of the introductory chapter. The model shows that readers' performances reflect the interaction of their levels of competence and motivation with the way material is organized and written.

From Chapter 2, The Reader's Performance

'Readability' can be defined either formally (as in a dictionary) or operationally (in terms of reader performance). An operational definition is helpful when reviewing studies of the effects of readability. Such studies vary written material in terms of **how said** (style) but not **what said** (content). Measures of reading efficiency, acceptability, and comprehension (and learning) then demonstrate any effects upon reader performance. To summarize briefly, changes in the readability of material consistently affect efficiency and acceptability. They do not consistently affect comprehension, being most effective with readers of average (or lower) knowledge and motivation levels.

From Chapter 3, The Reader's Level of Competence

Mature readers (in skill, not necessarily age) can be described as those whose **brains** help their eyes more than their **eyes** help their brains. As they read, they develop expectations of what is to come, so that their eyes need only pick up minimal cues from which their brains 'make sense'. The visual information is picked up in brief fixations, with the details typically remaining in 'working memory' only about 20 to 30 seconds before the general ideas pass into 'long-term memory'. Reading can be described as a process of reasoning, and readers' levels of competence relate to their knowledge of the language, education/experience, and interest in the reading. Expert writers take readers' competence into account as they proceed.

From Chapter 4, The Reader's Level of Motivation

Readers behave according to a general principle called least effort – or, more descriptively, 'expected effort' necessary for 'expected reward'. Consequently, their reading may vary from 'reading to learn' to 'reading to forget' (i.e., be diverted) – in fact, may go beyond this from overcompensation for very difficult writing, at one end, to casual perusal at the other. Motivation is likely to be greatest when interest is aroused, knowledge is great, and the stakes are high. When reading conditions also permit readers to compensate for the difficulties they are meeting, performance tends to be very good. A writer can do one or both of two things to encourage reading: raise the level of reward to be expected from reading a piece of writing, or reduce the effort necessary to read it.

From Chapter 5, Outlining and Organizing for Readability

Many writers have trouble getting started on a writing task, particularly when it is sensitive, long, or complex. Starting with an outline can be helpful for several reasons. This not only gets some words on paper, but also emphasizes logical organization and encourages writer-reader co-operation – 'writing with the reader in mind'. The chapter presents ten points to consider when outlining, with the understanding that different writers and different writing tasks determine which ones and how many can be helpful at a particular time. The rationale for many of the points grew from research on how readers comprehend what they read, described in the remainder of the chapter.

From Chapter 6, Writing and Rewriting for Readability

Research suggests that changes in coherence (or cohesiveness) and organization, as well as in words and sentences (preferably altered together), may make writing more readable. 'Coherence' refers to what links sentences to each other, while 'organization' refers to how all sentences relate to the central theme or themes. Readers tend to **recall** better when writers present information:

1. in cause-effect and contrast arrangements rather than in list arrangements;

2. as straightforward (i.e. explicit) relationships rather than those requiring inferences (i.e., implicit);

3. in parallel constructions (i.e., with parts of a sentence parallel in meaning also parallel in structure), rather than in non-parallel constructions;

4. with repeated words and ideas, rather than words which occur only once and ideas which are novel;

5. tied to a reader's prior knowledge, rather than not tied to a reader's prior knowledge; and

6. in main ideas, rather than in details.

Effective word changes involve 'content' words (nouns, verbs, adjectives, adverbs, pronouns, and numbers) more often than 'function' words (the other categories). Technical terms are an exception; defining them is better than trying to change them. Word changes which can affect readability include:

1. greater use of words with high frequency of occurrence or familiarity;

2. increased use of short words;

3. more frequent use of words with high (versus low) association-value;

4. greater use of concrete (as opposed to abstract) words;

5. increased use of active verbs (as opposed to nominalizations);

6. decreased use of unclear anaphora (words or phrases which refer to previous information);

7. wise choice of adverbs to multiply intensity of adjectives;

8. careful choice of context around difficult words;

9. use of expressions familiar to intended readers; and

10. avoidance of unnecessary words.

Three questions can help locate words that might need changing: Is the word long? Will intended readers understand the word? Is the word necessary?

The research on sentence changes is sometimes contradictory, and suggests that such changes not be overdone, since they can make writing **less** readable. Sentence changes which can affect readability include:

1. decreased length of clauses and sentences, especially where such conjunctions as **but**, **for**, or **because** are involved;

2. use of statements in preference to questions;

3. choice of affirmative rather than negative constructions;

4. increased use of active rather than passive constructions;

5. avoidance of self-embedded constructions; and

6. avoidance of constructions in which the words have high depth (or 'commitments' which the reader must store while reading a sentence).

The above changes suggest that Simple, Active, Affirmative, Declarative (or SAAD) sentences are most readable. Since they are also the most common form found in the English language, making writing more readable involves increasing their proportion in passages.

From Chapter 7, The Readability Level of Written Material

Judgements of the level of difficulty of texts can come from:

- individual writers themselves;
- the consensus of groups of readers;
- comprehension tests covering the texts; and
- readability formulas.

Formulas, though they measure only style difficulty and do that imperfectly, are surprisingly good predictors. Use them for **rating** only, however, and not for **writing**. 'Writing to formula' provides no assurance that readers will find the result as comprehensible as the formula value indicates. Instead, use a formula independently before and after rewriting, and only as a predictor of (or check on) readability.

Chapter 1

Introduction

Readable writing is written clearly enough for someone else to be able to read it with ease and understanding. *How to Write Readable English* provides information about both readers and reading, and suggestions for writing, intended to help writers reach this goal. Robert Graves and Alan Hodge expressed this theme well in the title of their book for writers, *The Reader Over Your Shoulder* (Graves and Hodge, 1944).*

The roles of the writer and the reader seem clear; why should there be a problem? Primarily because writing and reading are among the most complex skills a human learns – and goes on learning for much of a lifetime. Though research can now explain a great deal about these two processes, they are far from completely understood. The same may be said for speaking and for listening with comprehension, of course. Yet while almost all humans in all societies learn to speak and listen well enough to get along, many never learn to read with understanding, or to write clearly.

According to estimates, only around ten per cent of the

* The names and numbers in parentheses refer to items in the reference list.

world's languages have a written form at all, which helps
to explain the literacy problem in developing countries. A
much higher percentage of the heavily spoken languages
of the world have a written form; and yet the number of
illiterates is still growing yearly, even in many of the
countries using these languages.

But is literacy a problem in the **English-speaking**
world? Is it necessary, or even desirable, to pay so much
attention to **readable** writing? Yes, especially since 'functional literacy', or reading well enough to get along in
society, has now also become so heavily involved. That is
why readable writing has become increasingly important
in recent years.

One Concern – Increased Reading Demands

The amount of reading our technological society requires
for success – or even survival – has been growing steadily.
The Bullock report, *A Language for Life* (Department of
Education and Science, 1975) points to the ever-higher
premium placed on the ability to read within classrooms.
Outside, the demands appear, if anything, even greater.
Comparing job-related reading requirements for the last
three-quarters of a century or so provides dramatic evidence. The first-known airplane flight manual, for the
1911 Glen Curtiss 'Pusher', contained less than a page of
instructions (FAA Academy; original dated 1911). By
contrast, the US Navy's Cougar aircraft of 1952 required
1800 pages of documents, and the modern F-14 requires
260 000 pages (US Navy, 1979). The documents for such
a fighter alone now weigh more than the heaviest fighter
itself in World War II!

Much of the additional reading required of almost
everyone in a modern democratic society involves such
forms and documents as those for health, unemploy-

ment, and social security. As Waller points out, the British public considers such forms '. . . an obstacle course of gobbledygook, small print, and impenetrable procedures' (1984, p. 36). The American public, according to Bendick and Cantu (1978), reads and completes such forms with great difficulty and many errors. A survey by Murphy (1973) showed that American readers considered such documents and job-related materials to be among the most important reading they do in a typical day. Yet the survey also indicated that no more than one per cent of those surveyed reported difficulty with what they had read, at first suggesting that the importance of difficulty had been exaggerated. A follow-up, however, revealed that when possible '. . . people simply avoid materials they find difficult' (Focus: Learning to Read, 1978). This points to a related aspect of the reading problem.

Another Concern – Limited Reading Skills

Both the United Kingdom and the United States, despite compulsory public education, must deal with one or another troubling literacy problem. The British Broadcasting Corporation, for example, publishes a handbook for adult literacy tutors (Longley, 1975), and Adult Basic Education programmes for teaching reading to illiterates can be found in most large US cities. The magnitude of the literacy problem can be seen even when limited to functional illiterates, considered by UNESCO to be those who can read, but do so at a level below reading grade 5 (US), or adding 5, a reading age of 10 (UK). For example, a survey by the US Department of Health, Education and Welfare found that 20 per cent of Americans over 17 fell in this category (New York Times, 1977).

Readers with such limited skills cannot handle much of the reading required today. Sticht (1973), for example, found that even US Army cooks needed reading grade-level skills of 6.0 to 6.9 (reading age level 11.0 to 11.9) to read their job materials, and supply clerks 7.0 to 9.9 (12.0 to 14.9). Results like these argue for raising the reading skill limit specified for functional literacy, and such arguments can be heard. Yet a survey by Duffy (1976) found that 18 per cent of US Navy recruits, though high school graduates, actually read below an eighth-grade level (reading age level 13). And only recently has the decade-long decline in reading skills of US high school graduates begun to level off (American College Testing Program, 1979).

Can Today's Reading Problem be Solved?

This two-fold problem of increased reading demands and limited reading skills clearly calls for improved reading instruction, and attention is now becoming focused on this issue. But this approach offers, at best, a long-term solution, involving better reading theory as well as improved practice. The urgency of the need demands an immediate solution also, in the form of improved written materials. This means changing the difficulty of the style of writing so that readers will find it easier to read and understand.

Efforts have been made for many years to improve the clarity of writing. Graves and Hodge (1944) provided a notable example, with their 25 'principles of clear statement'. Strunk and White's influential little book, *The Elements of Style* (1979), went through three revisions between 1959 and 1979, and is still widely used today. Similarly, Fowler's highly regarded *Dictionary of Modern English Usage* (1974) appeared in an earlier edition and has remained an important desk reference. Sir Ernest Gowers also exerted widespread influence on writing practice with his several books, his most recent edition being *The Complete Plain Words* (1973). Rudolf Flesch published still other influential books, notably *The Art of Plain Talk* (1946) and *The Art of Readable Writing* (1950).

This drive for 'plain English' has intensified recently, as shown by the following items.

- Former US president Jimmy Carter gave this movement an official push with his executive order on 23 March 1978, requesting that regulations be 'written in plain English' and be 'as simple and clear as possible' (Carter, 1978).

- New York enacted a 'Plain English Law' in 1978 which requires that contracts and other consumer documents be 'written in a clear and coherent manner using words with common and everyday meanings' (New York State Assembly, 1978). Seven other states in the US had enacted similar laws by February 1982 (Plain Language Laws: Update, 1982) and two more were added by November of the same year (New Plain Language Laws, 1982). Furthermore, the legal problems predicted by opponents in the five years since New York's pioneer law was passed have not occurred (Plain Language Laws – Myth and Reality, 1982–83).

- Desirable readability levels have been established for military manuals (Kniffin, 1979) and insurance policies (Pressman, 1979), and proposed for consumer credit contracts (McDonald, 1979).

- Sir Derek Rayner pointed to the problem in his review of administrative forms (Rayner, 1982) and a related White Paper (United Kingdom, 1982) declared the British Government's intention to reduce the burden such forms impose on citizens and businesses.

- Britain has established a Plain English campaign complete with Golden Bull Plaques for unreadable writing (Britons Take Aim at Gibberish, 1982).

Can writing be made readable enough to solve the problems described above? The evidence for the value of readable writing has, in some cases, been very dramatic. For example, readability levels of newspapers and magazines may strongly affect their readership. Editor Donald R. Murphy (1947) found increases of 45 per cent to 66 per cent for more readable as opposed to less readable versions in 'split-run' experiments in a farm newspaper. Charles R. Swanson (1948), a journalism professor, subsequently showed that the more readable version of a newspaper article yielded the following gains over the less readable:

- 93 per cent in total paragraphs read;
- 83 per cent in mean number of paragraphs read; and
- 82 per cent in number of respondents reading each paragraph.

In a study made with US Armed Forces Institute (USAFI) materials and personnel, a close relationship was found between the readability levels of USAFI courses and the probability students would send in all of their lessons (Klare and Smart, 1973).

Revisions of the British postal claim forms for the unemployed, involving clear language and good design practice, raised the level of usable forms from an initial 20 to 30 per cent to a later 72 to 73 per cent (Lefrere, Macdonald-Ross, Waller, and Abbott, 1983).

If the value of readable writing is so great, why go any farther? The reading problems of the world, at least the English-speaking world, can readily be solved! The answer, as always, is not nearly so simple. Improving readability is important, but it is only part of the answer and can only be used effectively in some situations. To put it most simply, readable writing can help only those who read. Non-readers are excluded, but so are some readers: those not motivated enough to begin. Even some who begin a piece of writing are excluded: those who find it too long or at least dislike it for some reason. In such cases, readability alone is not the answer; in the case of the postal claim forms, for example, other characteristics besides readability of style were also changed, and trial tests were run. So the critical questions concern where, when, and how readable writing can be of help, which are major issues in this handbook.

Two Questions: Prediction and Production

Most of the research on readable writing concerns prediction. The question is: how can you, as writers, **predict** how readable a piece of writing is likely to be for intended readers? There is a second question: how can you, as writers, **produce** writing that will be readable to intended readers? Prediction is not easy, with writing as complex as it is. But compared to production – to **writing** – it is much easier. There are several reasons for this.

Researchers who wish to predict how readable a piece of writing is can be content to look for 'index' variables, or elements, in language. They want to find simple elements of style whose counts reflect difficulty. Most of the large body of research on readability has centred on this question. A consequence has been the development of well over 200 'readability formulas' designed to predict the readability level of a piece of writing.

Researchers who wish to produce readable writing, on the other hand, must look for 'causal' variables in language. They want to find elements whose change actually makes writing easier or harder for readers. Unfortunately, text (or prose generally) is difficult to experiment with. One problem is discovering what can be changed usefully. Even when found, there is the added problem that the changes may result in stilted prose, or may be trivial.

Producers of readable writing may, when experimenting, 'hold variables constant' which are of great importance to a reader and may propose variables of dubious value to a writer.

Fortunately, however, some new research promises aid in understanding the writing process itself, and how writing can help or hinder readers. This 'process' approach examines the kind of cognitive (thinking) activities writers go through while composing; the earlier 'product' approach examined only the composition. Both of these complementary approaches can offer valuable suggestions for readable writing, suggestions which have been incorporated in this handbook. 'Text analysis' provides a good example. This product-oriented research attempts to describe how readers comprehend – and where and why they may fail to do so. Research on coherence in the field of linguistics and cognition in the field of psychology form its basis. A major focus is on the co-operation between the author and the reader, emphasizing what the author can do to lead the reader to draw the right inferences and arrive at correct interpretations. This research will be put to use in later chapters where it is appropriate, particularly Chapter 5 on Outlining and Organizing for Readability and Chapter 6 on Writing and Rewriting for Readability. But it is still new and tentative; many unanswered questions and contradictions remain. Why not, then, turn to the many writers who have written about their craft over the years? Their experience has led to some shrewd suggestions. Anyone familiar with Gower's *The Complete Plain Words* (1973) or Strunk and White's *The Elements of Style* (1979) will recognize this. Another personal favourite is a chapter of Bertrand Russell's called 'How I Write' (1961). He suggests:

1. avoiding a long word when a short one will do;
2. putting some qualifications, when many are needed,

into separate sentences rather than into one sentence; and

3. keeping the beginning of a sentence from leading the reader to expect something contradicted by the end of it.

Much research as well as good practice has stemmed from such sources. Cleverly worded suggestions stick in one's mind well enough to be around when needed. A good example comes from *The News Letter* of The Ohio State University, by way of the *Education Reporter* (1970).

> Rules for writing: Don't use no double negative. Make each pronoun agree with their antecedent. Join clauses good, like a conjunction should. About them sentence fragments. When dangling, watch your participles. Verbs has to agree with their subjects. Just between you and I, case is important too. Don't write run-on sentences they are hard to read. Don't use commas they aren't necessary. Try to not ever split infinitives. It's important to use apostrophe's correctly. Proofread your writing to see if any words out. Correct speling is esential.

Many writers have written about the writing process, and have made many suggestions for clear writing. An examination of 15 books, for example, turned up 156 such ideas, even after grouping them together as well as possible when they seemed to be saying the same thing (Klare, undated). No writer could possibly keep such a large number in mind while writing, of course, even if all were equally valid. They are not; in fact, some actually contradict others. These contradictions arise partly from the complexity of the English language, and partly from the different audiences and purposes the writers had in mind; but these explanations help a writer very little when actually beginning to write.

Why, then, **another** publication? Here are the reasons.

1. *This handbook concentrates on readability in writing.* It does not pretend to cover the grammar, spelling, and punctuation a writer needs to know. It cannot, in other words, take the place of the usual desk reference books. Good possibilities, if you want such books, are *Dictionary of Modern English Usage* (Fowler, 1974), *Usage and Abusage* (Partridge, 1973), *Harbrace College Handbook* (Hodges and Whitten, 1977) or the paperback *Harper's English Grammar* (Opdycke, 1977).

2. *The suggestions in this handbook are intended for writing the purpose of which is to inform or instruct.* There are many other possible purposes for writing: creation of a mood, poetic statement, mystery, etc. The suggestions will be inappropriate for many of these.

3. *The handbook presents a view of how the mature reader reads.* The term 'mature' refers to the fact the reader is no longer a beginner in reading; it does not refer to age as such. This description provides background for many of the handbook's suggestions and why they work.

4. *The suggestions themselves are, as far as possible, based upon recent research in psycholinguistics, text analysis, composition, and readability.* These related fields are growing rapidly and changing as new research complements, alters, or even contradicts the old (a personal collection of relevant references in the above areas is well over 1500 in number, most of them published within the last ten years). There are several consequences of this approach:

    a. The suggestions should be considered as **suggestions**, not rules. Sometimes they will not apply, and can even be detrimental. The complexity of the English language would make this so even if the rapid growth in the source fields did not. Together

they emphasize that these may be the latest suggestions (for a time, at least), but not the last words.
Each writer must decide when they are inappropriate, as well as when they fit.

b. The suggestions in the handbook are limited in
scope by the available research; many important
considerations in writing are not included because
research on them is lacking.

5. *The handbook is 'applied' in approach.* Users and
evaluaters of an early draft felt that too much
philosophizing discouraged the reader. Theory has
been included only when it can help to clarify practice.

6. *The handbook evolved largely from a simple model of reader
performance.* Figure 1 presents this model.

The model, based on a thorough review of the research
literature (Klare, 1976), suggests that the performance of
a reader depends upon more than just the level of readability of material. The content of the material also plays a
part, as do the reader's levels of competence and of
motivation.

Figure 1   A Model of Reader Performance

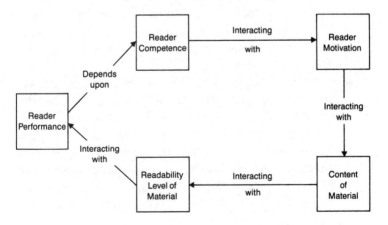

Each of these factors serves as subject-matter for a chapter in the handbook, and provides the organization for the chapters.

- Chapter 2 covers *the performance of readers*, e.g., their speed of reading, comprehension, and acceptance of what they are reading. Defining writing as readable only when it is readable to an intended reader (Klare, 1963) summarizes this chapter well.
- Chapter 3 describes *how the mature reader reads*, noting the limitations imposed by sensory memory, short-term memory, and long-term memory. Since what the reader already knows constitutes a major determiner of competence, Paul Kolers' statement (1969) that 'reading is only incidentally visual' provides a good summary for the chapter.
- Chapter 4 discusses *the range of reader motivation* from casual perusal to 'overcompensation'. William S. Gray's observation that this range may run all the way from 'reading to learn' to 'reading to forget' is an apt description.
- Chapter 5 takes up *outlining and organizing the content* to be communicated, based upon a modern 'text analysis' approach. Though not fully developed yet, this way of looking at writing can, in the words of Walter Kintsch (1979, p. 13) '. . . provide the practitioner with another set of intuitions about comprehension processes . . .'.
- Chapter 6 suggests *techniques for readable writing*, both at the first draft stage and later during the rewriting or editing process. How each writer may use such notions depends upon the individual needs and judgements at the time. That wry definition of an editor as one who substitutes his or her prejudices for those of the writer underlines the subjective nature of the process of writing readably.

After all, as another definition goes, editors are only humen!

● Chapter 7, a companion to Chapter 6, concerns the appropriate use of methods to assess *the readability level of a piece of writing*, with special attention to readability formulas. Robert Gunning's comment that formulas are for rating, not for writing, sums up the message of the chapter.

Throughout this handbook, the emphasis continually returns to the point that extra effort in writing readably can help each of our readers. As Edmund Berkeley once put it, 8 hours of a writer's time might well save 10 000 readers a total of 10 000 hours of time!

Chapter 2

The Reader's Performance

Formal and Operational Definitions of Readability

The term 'readability' has both formal and operational definitions. The formal is a dictionary-type definition, useful for a quick description. *Webster's New World Dictionary of the American Language* (Guralnik, 1970) says something is readable if it is 'interesting or easy to read'.

The operational definition tells how readability affects readers. How does a reader's performance change when reading something that is more readable as opposed to something less readable? A definition of this type is of special importance to a chapter called 'Reader Performance'.

Before defining readability this way, however, we need to consider several points. When we make a change in the readability of a passage to observe its effect upon reader performance, what kind of change do we mean? We must avoid changing **what** is said, or content, as much as possible. Instead, we change only **how** it is said, or style variables, such as familiarity or concreteness of the words used, sentence complexity, clarity in pronoun reference, coherence (degree to which a text 'hangs together'), etc. These changes will be discussed more fully in the later chapters; the point here is that unless we change only style variables, we are unable to tell what caused the changes in the readers' performance or even if they are still learning what they should be learning.

Some writers have argued that words cannot be changed without also changing meaning; others have argued that they can. Some synonyms or synonymous phrases may well introduce minor changes in meaning, but this is not usually a serious concern; only clear-cut changes in meaning need be avoided. The English language, fortunately, is particularly rich in synonymous words and phases. In addition to the two major streams of words, those of Latin and those of Anglo-Saxon origin, English has borrowed words rather freely from other languages.

Sentence changes can also often be made with little or no change in meaning; 'transformational grammar' has been particularly helpful in describing the various sentence forms. Text analysis offers a writer some insights on how to help readers draw those inferences needed to comprehend a piece of writing, yet without modifying meaning and intent. Consequently, we can assume that changes in **how** something is said (structure) need not significantly change **what** is said (content).

Changes in Reader Performance

With the structure-content distinction made, we can turn to the kinds of changes research has led us to expect in reader performance. At least two dozen methods of measuring performance changes have been used. The more common methods are listed under four major categories below.

1. **Reader efficiency.** The most common measure is reading speed in number of minutes or seconds for a passage of given length. Number of visual fixations or regressions may be used, but the equipment needed usually rules these out. Some research workers, however, do use such measures as bases for inferring comprehension (Carpenter and Just, 1981) or combine them with recall scores to get a refined index of efficient comprehension (Kintsch and Vipond, 1979).

2. **Reader acceptability.** This is shown either directly or indirectly by readers. The direct measure is most often a judgement by readers of whether passage A or passage B (or C or D) is easier (or easiest) to read.

   Indirect measures take several forms. In comparing magazine or newspaper articles, the most common method of measurement is readership. The comparison is usually made in a 'split-run' where one sample of readers gets one version of the material and a second sample another. Number of readers of each (determined by an interview or similar arrangement) is the index of interest. Sometimes a method is used involving reader 'persistence'. In magazine or newspaper articles, the measure usually involves depth of readership – how far into the material the reader reads. In correspondence course material, the measure may be the number of students who complete lessons and/or entire courses. Acceptability is a good measure to use in 'free-reading' situations, where there is little or no pressure to complete material. Most adult reading is of this sort, rather than a formal reading situation.

3. **Reader comprehension.** The measure most often used here is the common objective (usually multiple-choice) question. Recently, 'cloze' procedure has become popular because of its relative simplicity. A cloze passage is one in which every nth word (almost

always every 5th word) has been deleted and replaced by standard-sized blanks which readers are asked to fill in. Cloze scores on a passage are usually quite highly related to multiple-choice scores.

A different kind of measure involves the time a reader needs in order to read and verify the truth or falsity of a statement or to read about and carry out a task requested in a statement or paragraph. The presumption is that the more readable version yields shorter times than the less readable.

A final measure worth mentioning is paraphrase. Here readers give the meaning of a sentence or paragraph 'in their own words'. This method is seldom used except in translation studies because paraphrases are difficult to score.

4. **Reader learning and retention.** This category is sometimes included under comprehension, but the measures used are different enough to be separately placed. Furthermore, as one writer says, it is possible to learn a string of words without comprehending them, but comprehension helps. Similarly, it is possible to comprehend a string of words without retaining them, though comprehension improves retention in most instances. The most common measures of learning and retention are recall (i.e., memorization) and recognition (indicating whether or not something has been seen before).

There are two reasons for presenting these categories of measures. First, to discuss (below) the kinds of reader behaviour most likely to be affected by changes in readability. Second, to provide background for discussing how to make changes in readability in following chapters.

Reviewing the many studies of the effectiveness of readability in changing reader performance yields the following general conclusions.

1. *In almost all cases, improved readability results in greater reading efficiency, whether measured by time or eye-movement measures.* Most of us, as readers, tend to be rather inflexible in the rate at which we cover lines of print (except, of course, when we scan, skim, or search for particular items). We typically cover more readable material faster than less readable, however, for several reasons.

   a. More readable words tend to be shorter than less readable (for reasons to be discussed in Chapter 6). Therefore, a more readable passage tends to be read faster than a less readable passage with the same number of words.

   b. Studies with precise visual instruments show that more readable words are perceived (recognized) faster than less readable words of equal length.

2. *In almost all cases, improved readability results in increased reader acceptability.* With direct measures (judgements), readers are quite capable of distinguishing highly readable from highly unreadable material. They must certainly make a similar judgement when indirect measures are used, resulting in greater readership and persistence in the case of more readable materials. Since there is considerable competition for the reader's time – such as TV, radio, or other reading materials – ease of reading becomes a major determiner of behaviour.

3. *In many cases, improved readability brings increased comprehension, but not in all.* The reasons seem to lie chiefly in motivation, the circumstances of the reading, and how much of the information in the passage is already known. If motivation is very high and time is available, a reader will compensate for material that is low in readability through greater effort. When motivation

is lower, and/or time is limited, more readable material brings increased comprehension compared to less readable material. Similarly, readability has less effect when a reader already knows a great deal of what is covered in a passage prior to reading it. The model of reader performance in Chapter 1 contains the connecting phrases 'depends upon' and 'interacting with', for just such reasons.

4. *Only a few studies of the effect of readability on learning and retention are available.* They suggest that learning is affected in much the same way as comprehension; in fact, what can be recalled is typically related to how well it was understood in the first place.

The question to keep in mind is what you as a writer are interested in. Efficiency and acceptability are more consistently affected by changes in readability than are degree of comprehension and learning. In Chapter 3 we will look at how this general conclusion is affected by differences in reader competence, and in Chapter 4 how it is affected by differences in reader motivation. In Chapter 5 we will examine ways to plan for improved readability, and in Chapter 6 how to change language variables for this purpose. The effects upon readers will be summarized in terms of the measures described in this chapter.

Chapter 3

The Reader's Level of Competence

Writers agree that knowing more about their readers can help them to produce informative writing that is more readable. Surprisingly, few books on writing say much about readers and how they read. Yet this is necessary to understanding or evaluating reader competence.

Why is information on readers and reading not given? Not because none is available; a recent survey found over 15 000 reading studies. Perhaps it is **because** of the information; there seems too much to make sense of. The temptation may be to visualize so complex a picture of this process that it cannot be helpful.

The process **is** highly complex, but certain observations useful to writers can now be made reliably. But even then, just providing selected information does not mean that writers will use it. In fact, one thorough study (Atlas, 1979) shows that many will not. Besides knowing the needs of their readers, writers require ways of translating that knowledge into action (Flavell, 1974). This chapter attempts to provide the most relevant information for users of this handbook by:

● describing how reading proceeds, and
● focusing on the mature reader.

The term 'mature', as mentioned in the first chapter, refers to level of reading skills rather than to age. The beginning reader is excluded, because such a reader has additional problems not faced by the experienced reader.

The description to follow covers certain long-known facts about reading, but also brings in recent interpretations that have proved useful. John Carroll (1970) provides an excellent traditional research-based view of reading, Frank Smith (1982) adds an interesting information-oriented view, and Anderson and Pearson (1984) propose a 'schema-theoretic' view that is rapidly gaining adherents. If this disagreement in viewpoints seems surprising, or even disconcerting, remember that the reason lies not only in the complexity of reading behaviour, but also in the progress being made in understanding it. A brief review here cannot, of course, cover the known facts in detail; instead, emphasis has been placed on information that helps to explain reading as a process. Additional information about reader competence follows, along with a statement of the implications of the chapter for writers.

How Mature Readers Read

What kinds of movements are your eyes making as they move along a line of print like this? Though it may seem they are moving along smoothly, they actually are not. Instead, they are making a series of brief pauses, with quick movements between. If you want to observe this, have someone hold a book near eye level and read the top line silently while you watch that person's eyes carefully over the top of the book.

The 'fixations' of the line typically last about a quarter of a second. Only during these pauses is anything seen clearly; vision during the in between movements is unclear, and we learn to ignore what is seen. Another thing we learn to ignore is the material above and below the line we are reading. We **must** do this, since the 'visual field' is roughly circular and we see a good deal (as a child does) that would otherwise be distracting.

What we do see clearly, in the central part of our fixation, is typically from one to three or four words. How many depends, among other things, on their length, their familiarity to us, the light on the page, and our visual apparatus (if we are severely handicapped). We also get a **general impression** of several words, even though we cannot see them clearly.

We do not need to see all the words clearly to recognize them, however. How clearly we need to see them, and even how much of them we need to see, depends to a large degree on how often we have seen them in the past (an important consideration for writers). We also tend to 'fill in' what is not clear from the sense of the sentence, associations based upon previous words, and the like. Furthermore, even the fragmentary impressions are helpful. We get information about word length and word shape that helps us eliminate some words as impossible and consider others as more probable. Our next fixation, when we actually have these words in clear view, thus becomes more efficient.

What we actually 'see' is not well understood. We are often not conscious of the spelling or phonetic values of the words, for example. Yet we do see important cues or 'distinctive features' of some kind. We seldom confuse *hop, pop, cop,* and *mop,* for example. The beginning and ending letters seem especially well noted, and the ascender in 'h' and the descender in 'p', for example, act as cues. But we do not concentrate on letters (except in such special activities as proofreading), or even on the general shape of the word as such. The most important things seem to be how often we have seen particular words before and how competent we are as readers – in such cases, minimal cues are needed. We then say we have a good 'sight vocabulary' or that we have good 'immediate word perception'.

If we have *not* seen a word before, of course, this procedure changes somewhat. We *do* have to pay attention to letters, and to our knowledge of phonetics and spelling. This process of 'mediated word perception' often then permits us to do a good job of pronouncing new words. As Carroll points out, we realize that the strange word **dossal** rhymes with *fossil* and the unfamiliar **latescent** is pronounced like *fluorescent* rather than **late** and **scent**.

We pay more attention to subjects of sentences than to objects, and in general to words occurring early in the sentence. We also tend to pay more attention to content words than to function words. The term 'content' refers to nouns, pronouns, verbs, adjectives, adverbs, and numbers; 'function' refers to articles, conjunctions, preposition, and interjections. (The same word may, occasionally, be a content word in one context and a function word in another.)

All of this, for the mature reader, may take place very rapidly during a brief fixation. Moving left to right, we typically take about two such fixations per inch. This does not include some brief adjustment fixations we may take, and there are rather wide differences in fixation patterns and in rate and accuracy of comprehension.

What is seen during a fixation remains briefly as a visual image in what is called 'sensory memory' or 'sensory register'. Research psychologists typically speak of three memory systems, with sensory memory followed by 'short-term' (or 'working') memory and then by 'long-term' (or 'permanent') memory. Though this breakdown is not universally accepted, most psychologists do follow it, and it is particularly useful for explaining reading behaviour, as noted below. (Kagan and

Havemann, 1976, provide a short, readable description of the memory systems; Ellis and Hunt, 1983, provide up-to-date details.)

Visual images that reach sensory memory quickly decay under ordinary circumstances. Though the actual duration of the image varies somewhat (depending upon lighting and other factors), the typical length is approximately one-quarter second. That this value agrees with the duration of a typical fixation is more than coincidental. We need only about the first one-tenth second of a fixation to perceive information during reading, yet do not go on to a new fixation until about one-quarter of a second has passed. If we were to go on sooner, the visual images would tend to interfere with each other (which indicates why 'speed readers' skim and do not simply fixate faster.)

Once the visual image fades, the information is lost unless it is transferred to the next of the systems, short-term memory. This so-called 'working memory' stage lasts about 20 to 30 seconds, depending upon the circumstances of stimulation. Unless we repeat or rehearse what is in short-term memory it disappears, leading George Miller (1964) to compare it to a leaky bucket. This may seem unfortunate, yet there are advantages also. If we remembered everything at this stage we would be in trouble, since working memory holds only **about** four to seven separate items (depending upon their nature).

You can see that such a system exists by observing the 'eye-voice span'. Ask a friend to read a text aloud, with a warning that you plan to turn off the light being used unexpectedly, but that your friend should continue speaking as long as possible. Usually four or five words are uttered after the light goes out, because your friend's eyes have been that far ahead of his or her voice, with the words being held in short-term memory.

Much of the forgetting we do at this stage, then, appears

to be deliberate. But we do not wish to forget everything. Sometimes we want to retain information in its exact form, such as when we look up a telephone number and then go to dial it. We may not have to repeat it to ourselves if the book lies next to the telephone, but if we have to go even as far away as a booth this may become necessary. And if we plan to do several things **before** dialling, we will certainly have to repeat, or rehearse it. If we can 'recode' the number on some basis, however, such as its similarity to a well-remembered address or well-known date, we may be able to remember it with little effort and, in fact, retain it for a long time. Another term for this process is 'chunking', i.e., grouping items together in some highly meaningful way so they will act as one unit instead of seven or eight.

New information cannot generally enter short-term memory without 'bumping out' old information because of the limited capacity mentioned above. This process occurs over and over again as we read. Before it happens, however, we usually transfer the general meaning, or 'gist', into long-term memory. There seem to be few capacity limits on this system, but there are some other kinds of limits.

- Information enters long-term memory rather slowly – one estimate places the rate at only one item every five seconds or so.
- Details filter out in the process – we seldom remember the exact words of a long text we have been reading unless we have rehearsed them thoroughly.
- Only certain items enter – those which can become associated with relevant pieces of information already in long-term memory.
- Only certain items can be retrieved – though long-term memory appears to be an almost permanent

storehouse of information, we cannot always gain access to particular items.

These characteristics of long-term memory help to explain one of the dominant processes in reading. We appear to develop, as we read, 'expectations' or hypotheses of what is to come. The perceptual, meaning, syntax (sentence), and coherence cues lead us to expect certain ideas, if not words, to follow. If what we expect is confirmed by following fixations, we go on reading rather smoothly. If not, we adjust our fixation or focus, or even return to the area of a previous fixation (called 'regressing'), before moving forward again. Generally, left-to-right predictiveness seems to be quite important in our processing of sentences.

One thing we as readers do not like is to get either too much or too little information at a time. If it comes too fast we are likely to be frustrated; if it comes too slowly we are likely to be bored. Unfortunately, there is no good way to describe how to stay within such limits. We can get an intuitive notion, but a clearer description will have to wait for a better understanding of 'comprehension'.

Comprehension and Competence

You might think that, for all the years people have been discussing and teaching comprehension, they could by now at least agree on a definition. They cannot. In fact, if you review a set of such definitions without a distinguishing title, you usually find it easier to gain some reliable knowledge about the authors than about comprehension as a process. But progress in understanding comprehension continues to be made, and much faster in recent years. In Chapter 5 one point of view that can be of special help in the writing process will be discussed.

Something can also be said here about the **general**

effects of comprehension in the reading process. We know it may affect the number and rate of fixations, and particularly regressions. In addition to the 'plain sense' of a message that we get almost immediately, we also more slowly comprehend the implications of the message – draw inferences, judge truth or falsity, determine acceptability. Finally, we tend to remember sentences from the beginning and end better than those from the middle of a passage.

Beyond this, as we read larger amounts of material, we gradually build up a meaningful whole from what we have been taking in. Reading is thinking or, better yet, reasoning. The pioneer psychologist, Edward L. Thorndike, recognized this over 60 years ago when he launched the first real study of comprehension. It is this processing that permits us to read with sense. As Carroll says, we know that sometimes the word **read** should rhyme with **bead**, but that in another context it should rhyme with **bed** – the meaningful message we have been constructing in our heads tells us which is which, not our eyes. Smith describes the proper emphasis by saying that the brain tells the eye more than the eye tells the brain.

Anderson and Pearson present a still more sophisticated view in saying that we comprehend something when it fits into 'slots' in the 'schema' (or meaningful whole) relevant to what we are reading. A schema is defined as an 'abstract knowledge structure'. It is abstract in that it summarizes what is known through a variety of related experiences; it is structured in that it relates the component parts of the experience. For example, our knowledge of tense tells us that if the process of reading is continuing, the word 'read' will rhyme with 'bead'; if the process is over, it will rhyme with 'bed'. Of course, our schemata become far more complex than that. We may come to know that when in the UK, we pronounce the name of the city of Reading like 'bedding', whereas if we are in the

US, we pronounce the name of the city of Reading like 'beading'. And so on to much more elaborate schemata of many diverse kinds.

With this very brief look at how the mature reader reads, we can turn to the question of the reader's competence. It appears to depend heavily upon the following factors.

1. **The reader's knowledge of the language to be read.** Without a thorough knowledge, especially if it is a first language, the brain cannot build up the background for its contribution to the reading process, and reading occurs only very slowly and haltingly. We all too easily forget that even beginning readers are already accomplished speakers. If, for some reason, they are not, reading suffers.

2. **The reader's level of education.** In general, the higher the level of schooling a reader has reached, the better the reader, at least up to college age. Level of education is, however, as much an **index** of reading competence as a cause. More years of schooling expose a reader to particular words and word constructions many additional times, so he or she reads the words and sentences faster than a reader with fewer years of schooling. Such a person knows the meanings of more words and word combinations, also, and so reads with greater comprehension. But both effects **could** come from extensive reading by a person with relatively little formal education. In this sense, level of education is only an index of competence, but a very useful one because most persons with little formal education are not wide readers.

3. **The reader's field of interest.** A reader tends to see words and phrases related to a field of special interest many more times than others that occur equally often

in the language. This results in faster reading and greater comprehension. Space does not permit a thorough discussion of specific reader interests, since they are so varied. These findings may be useful, however: adults like to read about themselves or someone like themselves, and they like to read in and about their professional or occupational area. They also like to read about health, personality, and human nature (how to get along with others, particularly). Peace has also long ranked high.

4. **The reader's background knowledge.** As noted, new items of information are more likely to enter long-term memory when they can become associated with relevant pieces of stored information. Thus, the more relevant information a reader has built up, the easier it is to comprehend and retain new information. We cannot easily separate the effects due to background knowledge from those due to special interest, since the two tend to go together. Someone with a special interest in a topic is likely to pick up more background knowledge related to that topic than a person with less interest in it. However, two persons with equal interest may have different degrees of experience and thus still differ in background knowledge.

Of what use is this discussion? Isn't the reader's level of competence just a guess, or a risky judgement at best, unless you have a test score? Test scores are usually hard for writers to get, even for small audiences; for mass publications, they are usually out of the question.

What can be done? Level of education usually provides a good rough estimate of a reader's level of competence. As noted, exceptions do occur, where the last school grade a reader has reached is not a good index. But since the level of difficulty of writing is usually also estimated in terms of grade level, a rough match between reader competence and difficulty level of writing is possible with this measure. (How to judge the difficulty, or readability, of writing will be discussed in Chapter 6.)

A recent study (Entin and Klare, 1985) illustrates the use of readers' level of education when looking at the effects on comprehension of several factors. High degrees of reader interest, reader background knowledge, and readability were compared to low degrees of these factors. Each factor separately, as well as in combinations, contributed to comprehension, with the highest scores when the writing was at the readers' grade level and the lowest when it was above their grade level.

Implications for Writers

What implications does this chapter have for writers? Here are some of them.

1. **Reading is a skill.** The reader who does not practise loses the skill even faster, usually, than the over-practised motor skills of skating or cycling. That is why many persons who have once learned to read, later in their lives become functional illiterates. Unless material at their level and of interest to them is available, they cannot or do not read and thus lose their skill. This is especially true for readers who have not progressed beyond fourth-grade level (reading age level 9). About all they can read are comic books; even newspapers are not generally satisfactory.

   Just as reading skill can be lost, it can also be strengthened. Material roughly at the reader's level of competence provides for this. Several factors complicate this simple picture, but they are best left for the next chapters. Most important, though, is that the level of difficulty of writing – and related information rate – should fit the reader's level of competence. The reader then gains skill rather than becomes frustrated.

2. **Writing can help the reader form 'expectations' of what is to come.** As Bertrand Russell said, do not let the beginning of a sentence lead the reader to an expectation contradicted by the end of it. The same may be said for larger units than sentences.

3. **Reading is only incidentally visual.** As a writer, focus more on helping the brain to understand than on helping the eye to perceive. That is, emphasize words and constructions a reader has had previous exposure to and experience with.

Chapter 4

The Reader's Level of Motivation

It is easy to forget when writing just how many kinds – or, rather, levels – of motivation readers have for reading. As noted in Chapter 1, William S. Gray's observations led him to believe that motivations may easily range from 'reading to learn' to 'reading to forget' (i.e., be diverted, such as when reading a light novel or mystery to relax at bedtime). Few bestsellers are written the way textbooks are written. Perhaps textbooks should not be written in as difficult style as they often are, but since readers approach novels and textbooks with different motivations, text-book writers can use a more difficult style.

The Principle of Least Effort

Perhaps the best way to look at the effects of motivation is through the 'principle of least effort'. This principle says that persons will expend the least amount of effort necessary to reach a given goal. That is something of an over-simplification, of course, because we do not always know which path will involve the least effort – or sometimes even what the goal is, very clearly. We usually have **some** idea of each, though, and can modify our behaviour if these ideas change. In other words, 'expected effort' will vary with 'expected reward'. For writers, this is made even clearer by the so-called Yerkes-Dodson law: the level of difficulty of a task that a learner will attempt varies with the level of motivation.

However stated, the principle does work and has wide application. O. H. Mowrer provided a good example. He and his wife (both psychologists) decided that they would see how their baby daughter's begging behaviour changed when their handling changed. At first, she would cry and hold up her arms when she wanted to be picked up. Her parents tried very hard to pick her up as soon as she did this. The crying rather quickly dropped out and only the arm-raising remained. They continued to respond just as soon as possible by picking her up. Next only one arm was raised; then only one hand; and, finally, only a finger was flicked. The little girl was responding with the least effort necessary to reach her goal of being picked up. What do you suppose happened when she was no longer picked up for her least-effortful response? She went back, of course, to her full response of arm-raising and crying.

George Kingsley Zipf, who named the principle of least effort and examined it thoroughly, has other more complex examples of its presence (Zipf, 1949), and the principle applies especially clearly to reading. One excellent example comes from a fair where three booklets on fruit growing and cultivation were prepared for free distribution. All covered the same topic, but differed in level of reading difficulty. One, intended for 4-H club members, was easiest to read; another, intended for fruit farmers, was hardest to read. The third, prepared for general farmers, was in between in difficulty.

Labelled piles were made of each booklet, and they were placed on a table where passers-by could pick them up. Each pile, at the start of the fair, contained a number of booklets proportional to the number of 4-H members, general farmers, and fruit farmers expected. Observers noticed, however, that all three categories of potential readers, after a bit of paging through, tended to select the 4-H version, and it disappeared first. Next went most of the general-farmer version, and last and least went the most difficult version of all, that intended for fruit farmers.

This principle of least effort is a powerful determiner of reading, but it says nothing specifically about the range of motivation to be found among readers. Nor does it say (to any extent, at least) how motivation can be managed.

We have already noted that motivation to read ranges from the desire to learn to the desire to forget, but actually the range is even somewhat greater, from 'overcompensation' at one end to 'casual perusal' at the other. Compensation can be defined readily by example. A study of some years ago looked into the effect of noise on typists' efficiency. One group of typists worked in a quiet room, one in a noisy room, but both on the same typing material. The two groups typed about equally well, in terms of amount of work done and errors made. The investigators were puzzled by this finding. Then someone happened to notice that the typists working in the noisy room seemed more tired at the end of the study. Effort indicators (springs) were then placed under the keys for a later study. As expected, the typists in the noisy room were using more effort to reach their level of performance than those in the quiet room. Those in the noisy room appeared to be trying to live up to their own standards of performance (it was a 'test', after all), and in order to do so had to 'overcompensate' for the noise.

As for compensation in general, how does it show up in reading? The reader may do any one or more of the following to compensate for difficulty.

- Reread the material one or more times.
- Use a dictionary, thesaurus, or other potentially useful aid.
- Get other material on the same subject in the hope of better understanding.
- Talk to other persons who are more knowledgeable.

Richard Kern, Thomas Sticht, and Lynn Fox (1970) found that the number of servicemen who would ask others for information depended upon the degree of difficulty they had with their reading material. We all do this on occasion; a common case is filling out income tax forms.

Readers can and will compensate for difficult reading when they are highly enough motivated to do so. The level of difficulty of a particular piece of writing becomes less important, then, compared to when motivation is lower. Even readers with little competence will struggle with it, but they welcome an easier task. As a writer, an extra hour of your time in rewriting can save readers many hours of their time, as pointed out earlier. If you want their good will, or hope they will read your writing again, an easy-to-read style is good insurance.

Writers, like testers of intelligence, always hope **their** particular readers have a very high level of motivation. Not only can this compliment them and make their job easier; greater understanding and/or higher test scores also result. Unfortunately, readers seldom have exceptionally high levels of motivation. Nor do they usually have very low levels of motivation when reading for information or instruction. A 'casual perusal' level occurs, for example, when a reader is paging through a newspaper or magazine, perhaps because of having nothing more engaging to do.

The level of difficulty of reading matter is important to a casual reader, but less so than the topic involved. If we do not find something that fits our interests or mood of the moment, or that is striking for some other reason, we may pass by even the most readable material. Note, however, that an easy reading style may hold even casually interested readers on material that a difficult reading style would turn them away from.

So, difficulty does matter for the casual reader. But it matters even more for that large group of readers between this extreme and that of overcompensation. Most readers fit somewhere in this middle category. Reading difficulty is important to them, especially important if what they are reading is long. Irving Lorge once made a study of the readability of consecutive issues of a digest. The editors seemed pleased at first by the work, but later became concerned when he pointed out that the circulation of each new issue was related to the readability of the previous issue. When readability scores were low, readership of the following issue was low also; when scores were high, readership went up with the next issue. As low scores touched the editors' pet articles in various issues, their concern turned to disenchantment and Professor Lorge's funds were stopped. He continued to compute the readability scores of the following issues for his own information, and found that a succession of low scores put the digest out of business.

The Effectiveness of Motivation

A number of other studies have shown essentially the same kind of result: the difficulty of writing does make a difference for the reader with average or lower motivation. What, though, can be done to determine motivation? What are the important factors? Researchers have been working on this question long enough to tell us that no easy answers are available, but a few findings do seem clear. Remember that a very high level of motivation, if it can be achieved, reduces the importance of the level of readability. The levels below this, on the other hand, increase its importance. Even when motivation is high, however, greater comprehension occurs in less time when reading more, as opposed to less, readable writing.

When is motivation to read likely to be high?

1. **When interest in the subject-matter is high.** Keeping readers interested – once they have decided they are willing to give a piece of writing a try – is therefore in order.

2. **When content knowledge is relatively high.** The word 'relatively' may seem out of place, but is included because readers are seldom interested in a piece of writing that tells them nothing (or very little) that is new. Too much new information, of course, also drives readers away as we saw in the last chapter. In the terms used earlier, information gain should be held to an intermediate level; either too much or too little turns readers away.

3. **When the stakes are high.** Researchers and testers have known this for a long time, which is why subjects are often told (or led to believe) that a given experiment or test will contribute to course grade, indicate intelligence, show ability, or whatever. Manipulating instructions in such a way is not easy unless the reader is in a classroom. Even then, the reader's **personal** stakes must be high if such instructions are to work.

Instructions designed to motivate the reader are likely to be helpful only when the testing situation is appropriate. An example comes from a personal review (Klare, 1976) of 36 experiments in which a more readable version of material was pitted against a less readable to see if the former would result in higher scores on a comprehension or learning test. Slightly over three-fifths of the studies produced positive results, while slightly under two-fifths were negative (usually producing nonsignificant differences in comprehension scores). Many of the studies were doctoral dissertations, and it was possible to get microfilm copies of them and study in detail what the experimenters had done (most reports of studies in scientific journals have too little detail for this).

Given the high stakes mentioned above, several of the following were also necessary if high motivation was to produce high scores on the less-readable versions.

1. The test was sufficiently sensitive to show experimental differences. As obvious as this may seem, some studies failed because the test appeared to be insensitive to differences in comprehension.

2. The time limits given to the subjects were lenient. Without the necessary time, the extra effort resulting from overcompensation was not likely to produce higher scores.

3. Re-reading of the experimental text was permitted. Where experimental conditions permitted only one reading, such high test scores seldom appeared.

4. Reference to the text was permitted while answering the comprehension questions. This is the way many reading tests are arranged, and higher scores result than when reference to the text is not permitted.

Implications for Writers

What relevance does all this have for us as writers? We cannot usually control motivation or the reading (testing) situation. We must, therefore, guess what our readers' situation is going to be. How much detail do they need to get from the writing? Will they probably have time to re-read? More important, are they likely to take the time to re-read? Will they usually have the written description around when they need to perform a task? Will they refer to it? Unless motivation is high, these questions are very important. It is all too easy, unfortunately, to assume a higher motivation for readers than they are likely to have.

What other implications for writing can be drawn from this chapter? Since the principle of least effort plays an important role in reading, a writer might well try to do one of the following.

1. **Raise the level of expected reward.** This can some-times be done by indicating the importance of what is being read, or its relevance to the reader's life. Two major studies of expert and novice writers (Hayes and Flower, 1980b; Atlas, 1979) showed that experts used a far more personal style than did novices, especially in opening paragraphs.

2. **Reduce the level of expected effort.** This approach is basically one of making writing more readable – easier to read. The next three chapters concern themselves with how to achieve this.

Chapter 5

Outlining and Organizing for Readability

Writers differ in how they approach writing because it is, after all, a very personal matter. Getting started can be very difficult, especially if the task is sensitive, or complex, or long. John Hayes and Linda Flower (1980b) have studied a number of writers in action, and have found that some try for a perfect first sentence or even a perfect first draft, while others get material down first and review later. But they also find (Flower and Hayes, 1980b) that the experience of writers rarely supports any tidy sequence of stages.

Because of this variety, comments on how to approach a writing job often have limited application. One suggestion that many writers can and do support, however, is to begin by developing an outline as a way of organizing their ideas (Flower and Hayes, 1980b) – and some even say that putting such words on paper helps in getting the writing process into gear. This suggestion, moreover, gains further support from a new and useful view of reader comprehension. That is to say, an outline can help to provide a logical organization which the reader can follow easily.

Writer-Reader Co-operation

The above arguments for outlining focus on the view that writers wish to help readers understand, and that readers, in turn, wish to understand. This so-called 'principle of co-operation' between writer and reader applies to most informative and expository writing. That **writers** do not always have understanding as a primary goal, at least, can be seen in many traditional legal documents and some modern literature. That **readers** do not always have understanding as a primary goal can be seen in proofreading and in searching for specific items in a list, to take two cases.

An important characteristic of writer-reader co-operation is that it forms a basis for readers to assume certain things about what a writer intends but does not actually say (Grice, 1975). Readers continually draw inferences based on their store of knowledge. They derive meaning both from what is said and what is not said. If a writer had to spell out every detail, both writing and reading would be inefficient.

In fact, writers can say too much, and have the opposite effect they intend. Consider readers who come across something that seems too obvious, something they could hardly have avoided assuming. The writer may simply have been making a special effort at clarity, but readers may not realize this and instead search for hidden meanings; else why would the writer have bothered to say something so obvious? Thus a writer's attempt to be 'perfectly clear', as former US president Richard Nixon liked to say, can sometimes even lead to the same kind of suspicious reception among readers that he got from many of his listeners.

There seems to be no certain way to say enough to help readers, yet not too much. As noted earlier, studies of the comprehension process have long shown reading to be reasoning. Not necessarily the formal type of reasoning found in the field of logic, but reasoning nevertheless (as the last part of this chapter will show). What a good outline can do is help the reader through the chain of inferences to the desired conclusions.

Asking writers to consider outlining may seem to imply that they need to get words on to paper at the first possible moment. Careful observations show quite the opposite. Writing is a goal-directed activity (Hayes and Flower, 1983), and preliminary planning may take up the bulk of a writer's time (Frase, 1981). Amount of time spent in planning, in fact, helps to distinguish more skilled from less skilled writers (Flower and Hayes, 1980a; Schumacher, Klare, Cronin, and Moses, 1984).

The planning period often consists largely of silently retrieving and mentally organizing information, and much of it may occur even prior to writing down any part of an outline. The actual amount of time will vary, both among writers and with the length and complexity of the writing itself. When material is technical, scientific, or legal, and when formal restraints are placed on its structure, research and planning time increase.

Knowing when to end the planning stage and begin the writing stage can also be troublesome. Inconsequential or even unpleasant tasks (pencil sharpening or even dental visits) can assume new importance or urgency. It is here that outlining can be a helpful bridge to writing itself.

Suggestions for Outlining

What does an outline, particularly one designed with the reader in mind, look like? To specify rules or standard procedures would be useless, since outlining (like writing) is an individualistic activity. To provide some suggestions may be useful, though, in uncovering steps worth trying. Sift through the following suggestions for those which may be of help in your particular writing circumstances.

1. Begin an outline with the thoughts you have in mind; order and organization can come later. Recording such seemingly random ideas can get you started and thus over the first hurdle. Even though writing is strongly goal-directed, Hayes and Flower (1983) found that goals are commonly modified as writing proceeds. (If you expect changes, you can be more flexible, at least in the beginning.)

2. Consider putting these bits of information on cards rather than regular sheets of paper. Such arrangement makes it easier to add, replace, and sort your ideas when necessary.

3. Include sources for your information as you go along, especially if you are doing technical or scholarly writing where you will need to provide references. This can save time in long or involved writing, because you may have trouble remembering them later.

4. Select the places for illustrations, tables, and figures if you plan to include any. Add a note (or a card) as you see where one of these could be of help to readers.

5. Arrange your ideas in what seems to be the most **logical** order. The term 'logical' is easier to use than to describe. Various writers, thinking mostly of fiction, have suggested chronological, psychological, procedural, and flashback possibilities, among others. Surprisingly, the choice can be easier for fiction than non-fiction – or expository – writing, because in fiction the 'story line' provides a framework. Some recent research does, however, provide a way to compare

several different possible organizations for non-fiction. Four types have been described and studied, in terms of how items of information have been presented (Meyer and Freedle, 1978):

a. *adversative,* with items contrasted;
b. *covariant,* with items presented in cause-effect relationships;
c. *response,* with items related in terms of problems and solutions; and
d. *attributive,* with items given a list-like pattern.

Listeners to passages organized with adversative and covariant structures remembered significantly more information than listeners to passages organized with attributive and response structures. Those who listened to the first two (adversative and covariant) also used these kinds of relationships in organizing their statements about what they recalled. This new line of research requires further exploration before more definitive statements can be made. However, Meyer and Freedle in their recent study (1984) did find support for the earlier work. Once again the adversative (here called 'comparison') and covariant ('causation') approaches provided for better recall than the attributive ('collection of descriptions'). The only difference from the earlier study was that the response approach ('problem/solution') also yielded better recall than the attributive. Despite this encouraging agreement in an entirely different study, general statements must await further research. For example, these studies emphasized recalling information. If reader acceptability (ease of reading) had been emphasized, a list-like structure may well have had advantages (Frase, 1981). Whatever organization you choose, these remaining suggestions may prove helpful.

6. Order items of information with at least these major thoughts in mind.

    a. Relate the members of a set to each other in a consistent way; this helps readers to see what belongs to the set or schema, especially in a long and complex text.

    b. Remember that readers must play an active role if they are to comprehend, learn from, and/or remember what you have written.

Some concrete suggestions for helping readers to play an active role have come from recent studies and are given below.

7. Keep these research-based ideas in mind as you follow the logical order you have selected.

    a. Choose the most descriptive titles and headings you can, whether for a memo or a longer piece of writing. Titles must usually be brief, and headings also – often only a word or two; within such limits, choose titles and headings which present your major concept or theme or 'gist'. The title of a long piece of writing represents a great deal of abstracting; but even such distilled concepts help, since readers can tie to them the information you present. Readers remember main ideas better than details, and main ideas stated in familiar and explicit terms prove especially helpful organizers for readers. The lack of such titles and headings, or poorly chosen ones, makes the job of readers more difficult. They may be misled at worst, or may comprehend and retain your information inefficiently at best (Bransford and Johnson, 1972).

    b. Keep your ideas in a 'hierarchical' (or degree-of-importance) order, so that readers can recognize and emphasize more important versus less important points. Hayes and Flower (1980a) report that many writers consciously organize their material as a hierarchy; they first identify major goals, then follow with subgoals under these major goals. Readers, similarly, make judgements concerning major and minor points in the normal course of reading, but you can help the process along by your organization and the cues you give.

c. Lead your reader from one idea to another in reasonable steps, i.e., make your writing cohesive from sentence to sentence. You may yourself easily make logical leaps from one point to the next because you know your material better than your reader. But a reader who cannot see a relationship must infer what you did not say, and when the leap is large this can lead to errors in understanding.

d. Repeat enough information so that your reader does not get puzzled, and have to go back to previous statements or sections of material as memory refreshers (Kintsch, 1979).

The theoretical bases for the above suggestions will be presented later in this chapter, and may help you see more clearly how to put these research conclusions into practice. It may help to say at this point, however, that you might have to sort your points (cards) *several* times before achieving a satisfying order or plan of organization.

8. Use a coding scheme which reflects order of importance. A common scheme makes use of both numbers and letters, and spacing or indentation as well. If you have used cards, you may wish to transfer the ideas to paper or computer printout at this stage for convenience. A partial outline might look like this, using a common coding scheme.

I.

   A.

      1.

         a.
         b.

      2.

         a.
         b.
         c.

   B.

      1.

         a.
         b.

      2.

II.   etc.

You may not wish to use the particular letters and numbers here; the degree of indentation can, by itself, reflect the degree of importance of the items.

You may, of course, want to use your own coding scheme, or you may be asked to use one that conforms to some special standard or format in your organization. If your writing will need to be presented in some special way (e.g., with specified centred or side headings, numbered paragraphs, etc.), you can save time by co-ordinating your outline scheme with this. Whatever scheme you use, your outline can help to indicate whether or not you have achieved the desired hierarchical, and in other ways logical, order.

9. Fill in details in the outline as they occur to you. The degree of detail will vary with different writers, and for different lengths and purposes in writing. Some writers, especially of instructional materials, develop a highly detailed set of objectives they wish readers to

achieve. The writing task then becomes highly structured. If you wish to consider this approach, a good source of information on developing objectives is Robert Mager's little book, *Preparing Instructional Objectives*, Second Edition (1975).

An even more detailed (and still experimental) approach has been developed by Bonnie Meyer in studying the organization of prose and its effects on memory (Meyer, 1975b). Her analysis of a passage looks much like an outline of the passage in its hierarchical structure, but unlike an outline it includes all the ideas in the passage. Making such an analysis can be extremely time-consuming, and has been used mostly for research.

Most writers proceed better with a less highly structured outline. Whatever the level of detail you choose, keep in mind that an outline is not fixed; make changes as you see the need for them. Continue to be flexible in your approach, if possible.

10. Look for added supporting evidence of the points in your outline when you feel it is important. Searches may take various forms: library research; requests for information from others; logical analyses; and possibly experimentation. This depends, of course upon the nature of your writing task.

The description here may imply that a writer following these outlining steps now can begin writing. A more appropriate way to put it is that a writer who has considered these suggestions is likely to be *better prepared to begin* writing than one who has not. This may be clearer after a brief look at the theory of reading comprehension which led to many of the points included above. This theory clarifies why writers must keep their readers – and their readers' limitations as information processors – in mind while writing. It helps to emphasize the importance of writer-reader co-operation.

You may wish to skip the remainder of this chapter at this time if the theory of comprehension does not interest you, or if the next chapter (Writing and Re-writing for Readability) interests you more. What follows formed the basis for many suggestions in the next chapter, however, so consider coming back to this section later if you skip it now.

Comprehension Theory

Walter Kintsch, with his associates and students at the University of Colorado and elsewhere, has developed the theory of comprehension relied upon most heavily in this chapter. Because this theory led to certain of the points in outlining just described, it will be presented briefly below. The general approach can be found in books and articles by: Kintsch (1974; 1979); van Dijk (1977); and the two authors in collaboration (Kintsch and van Dijk, 1978). Further details and research appear in: Kintsch and Keenan (1973); Kintsch and Vipond (1979); Miller and Kintsch (1980); and Kintsch and Yarbrough (1982).

Related information regarding expository (informative) text has come from a number of other research workers in this so-called 'text analysis' field. Bransford and his associates (Bransford and Franks, 1971; Bransford and Johnson, 1972; Bransford and McCarrell, 1974) have also been looking at problems of comprehension, with early emphasis on the importance of titles. Anderson and his associates (Anderson, Spiro, and Montague, 1977; Anderson and Pichert, 1978; Anderson and Pearson, 1984) have been examining the role of the reader's 'schema' in acquiring knowledge, with special attention to how perspective can influence what is recalled. Frederiksen (1975) and Meyer (1975a; 1975b) have been particularly interested in the semantic aspects of text, and have emphasized its hierarchical nature. Halliday and Hasan (1976) and Hobbs (1979) have given special attention to the cohesive aspects of text. Reder (1980) has shown that readers who 'elaborate' on (or embellish) a text during reading develop better long-term retention of its content. All of these writers, plus other text analysts, have helped our understanding of how we understand. (For a review of this complex and diverse area, see Reder, 1980, and Pearson and Camperell, 1981.)

Of all these writers, Kintsch provides the best integrated framework so far for helping writers to write more readably. Comprehension, as he describes it, involves more than the understanding of isolated words, phrases, clauses, or even sentences in a text. These elements must be organized into a coherent pattern before meaning becomes clear. This can best be seen by describing a 'text base' briefly. Suppose, for example, that a reader encounters this segment of a passage.

> A great black and yellow V-2 rocket 46 feet long stood in a New Mexico desert. Empty, it weighed 5 tons. For fuel it carried 8 tons of alcohol and liquid oxygen.

How and what kind of meaning grows out of reading these words?

Such a text, according to Kintsch, consists of a series of propositions. When properly structured, they form a text base. To describe how the structuring occurs, a few terms need to be defined and illustrated.

1. **A proposition** consists of a predicate, with one or more arguments. In print, it typically takes the form of a clause with a verb.

2. **An argument** is a concept. Though we use a word and/or its synonyms (typically nouns) to represent it conveniently, the concept itself is abstract.

3. **A predicate** can be thought of as a comment about an argument. In a text, some quality or characteristic is attributed to the argument.

Using the passage given above, the first argument is 'rocket'. The rocket is characterized as 'great', as 'black', as 'yellow', as a 'V-2', and as 'long'. 'Long' is itself further characterized as '46 feet'. The rocket is also described as having 'stood' in the 'desert', with 'desert' further specified as 'New Mexico' desert. Using Kintsch's shorthand method of respresenting arguments, this becomes the following, with propositions numbered, and with predicates preceding the arguments. To emphasize that the words merely represent the underlying abstract notions, they are capitalized. For convenience, arguments which consist of other propositions (as they may, when meaning builds up), are simply numbered rather than repeated. The first sentence appears as follows in this sort of representation.

1. (GREAT, ROCKET)
2. (BLACK, ROCKET)
3. (YELLOW, ROCKET)
4. (V-2, ROCKET)
5. (LONG, ROCKET)
6. (46 FEET, 5)
7. (STAND, ROCKET)
8. (IN, 7, DESERT)
9. (NEW MEXICO, DESERT)

This extended presentation covers only the first sentence of the brief passage above. Is it really necessary to understand how readers achieve meaning? Can the getting of meaning be all that complicated? It hardly seems so. But in saying that, we forget the years that have gone into making the process automatic for us. Evidence to show that the automaticity of the process grows can be seen in a recent study of beginning college writers versus mature writers (Schumacher, Klare, Cronin, and Moses, 1984). Much of a writer's thinking occurs during the inevitable pauses in the writing process; this study looked at the length of the pauses and the cognitive (thinking) activities carried out when the writer paused. As it turned out, beginning writers showed they were less highly automated in their thinking activities by pausing longer than mature writers yet also engaging in fewer cognitive activities during the pauses.

If this kind of automating of the writing process can be seen so clearly over several college years, it is easy to imagine how much more automating must have gone on in the much more complex processes of learning to read and write in the first place. Thus the complexity of Kintsch's representation does not seem so strange. And, as Kintsch points out, his view can help to clarify what has gone (and goes) into the business of comprehending, and how human limitations have determined (and still determine) how we achieve meaning. What does happen? Kintsch's theory combines the above analysis with the characteristics of human memory and human behaviour during reading (described in Chapter 3, as noted below).

Comprehension and Competence Reconsidered

To repeat briefly the material in Chapter 3, the following steps can be observed during reading. The eyes pick up one or more clear words on a page during a brief fixation, and hold them in visual memory for about a quarter of a second. The information passes into short-term, or working, memory, which can hold up to seven or so items (but more **related** words). The general idea, or 'gist', gained from these words then passes on into long-term memory. If readers become confused at some point, they must look back at an earlier part of the text to re-establish meaning. Such fixations, called regressions or 'look-backs', make reading inefficient.

How does Kintsch's theory explain this behaviour? As readers go through a piece of writing only a part of what is read can be held in working memory. As the example showed, the number of propositions grows rapidly even in seemingly simple text, and two dozen would usually be too many to work with directly. Somehow, readers must work with just a part of the text base at one time, and add it to a growing 'graph' or picture. As they proceed to the next section, they can carry along only a selected subset of the previous material, to which the new incoming part of the text base can be connected. This connection, or relation, 'makes sense' of the text.

A coherent or cohesive text helps readers to establish such connections easily. If they cannot relate a new segment to the current contents of working memory, they are in trouble. They must then search long-term memory to locate an idea from the previous text to relate to the new segment. This is called a 'reinstatement search', and, even if successful, reduces reading efficiency. Sometimes readers must actually regress visually or look back at an earlier part of the text to set up relations with previous material.

This interpretation of how we comprehend receives support from a study carried out from a different orientation (Britton, Westbrook, and Holdredge, 1978). Readable passsages produced better comprehension, according to the authors of this study, because they filled the 'cognitive processors' fully. Difficult passages, on the other hand, appeared to empty the short-term memory and other processor spaces. (Subjects reading the difficult passages showed they had cognitive capacity available by beginning to respond to a secondary task which those reading the easy passages did not respond to.) Readable text, then, did not involve reinstatements and was read more efficiently than difficult text.

What causes reinstatement searches by readers? The author might have been careless, for example, or the topic might have shifted. On the other hand, some readers may not have made an expected connection because of some kind of distraction. For whatever reason, coherence has failed; readers must now generate a 'bridging' inference to connect the new segment with the preceding text. Successful connections depend upon relevant knowledge and skill in drawing inferences. But even when successful, such inferences take time and make reading inefficient.

Kintsch calls the above activities 'microprocesses'. They can be seen most clearly in short paragraphs, particularly those with little supporting context. They can also be found in longer texts, along with additional activities Kintsch terms 'macroprocesses'. These processes deal with the overall semantic content of a piece of writing as seen in a number of propositions, and may involve transforming old propositions or creating new ones. These abstracting and summarizing activities result in the kind of 'schema', or knowledge structure, that enters long-term memory.

One question you may have concerns what propositions are selected for carry-over from short-term memory from one 'cycle' to the next. Though not completely clear, the evidence favours a combination of those that are 'superordinate' and recent. The term superordinate means, in effect, most important. Studies show that readers remember important information better than lower level details.

Why do readers retain important information better? First, because the skilful writer has usually emphasized it in the title of the text, in headings, and/or in summary statements. Second, because the argument in a string of propositions 'overlaps' or recurs; the argument ROCKET in the earlier analysis is an example. This repetition leads readers to remember this important concept better than other details. Third, because the information considered important by a particular reader may be determined to some extent by that person's store of knowledge and/or level of interest in a given topic. As studies show, readers with different perspectives may recall some of the same information, but also recall some different information from a given text.

Implications for Writers

To summarize, Kintsch's model of how readers comprehend text ties qualities in the text to abilities and limitations in readers. The traditional readability variables discussed in the next chapter, word frequency or familiarity, and sentence length or complexity, appear to affect reading time primarily. The arrangement of the propositions in the text base, on the other hand, appears to affect recall primarily. This arrangement determines the number of reinstatements of already processed propositions from long-term into short-term memory, and the number of bridging inferences readers must make. Thus, characteristics of readers enter the picture along with characteristics of the text. Since both reading time and recall contribute to the efficiency of comprehension, both characteristics also interrelate in determining whether writing will be readable.

What does a writer need to keep in mind when going from an outline to a readable text? Familiarity of words and complexity of sentences, of course, but also the arrangement of the propositions that readers must face. If particular readers must make a large number of reinstatement searches and/or bridging inferences, either because of limited ability or knowledge, or because a text lacks coherence, they cannot comprehend efficiently. Producing readable writing takes careful planning. The suggestions in the next chapter can help to promote the desired writer-reader co-operation in going from outlining to writing.

Chapter 6

Writing and Rewriting for Readability

This chapter presents suggestions for writing readably. They derive from research in psycholinguistics, readability, and text analysis, with special attention to the new 'process' approach to research in writing. Unlike **rules** of grammar, these **suggestions** can and do change as new research conclusions supplant the old. Use care in applying them; mechanical application may be as harmful as helpful.

These suggestions do not cover all the important components of writing, even of writing designed primarily to be readable. When writing or rewriting material to make it readable, you often need to consider such other variables as typography, graphics, or examples, and they are not discussed in this chapter. Available research limited the number of suggestions, because those presented here had to qualify as research-based. For that reason, only word and sentence suggestions appeared in earlier editions of this handbook, but research in text analysis later opened the way for suggestions on coherence and organization also. As noted earlier, recent research frequently looks at writing as a **process**; this new approach is reflected in this chapter (as well as, to some extent, other chapters) of this edition of the handbook.

What is new about this approach? As noted earlier, research centres on the thinking (cognitive) **processes** of writers while writing rather than on the **products** of their writing. Janet Emig's study (1971), most agree, began this new trend; most also credit the British team of Britton, Burgess, Martin, McLeod, and Rosen (1975) with the first large-scale work. Influential among the first research workers were Flower and Hayes, with Gregg and Steinberg's *Cognitive Processes in Writing* (1980) a significant early collection of papers. Notable recent books include those by Frederiksen and Dominic (1981), Nystrand (1982), Mosenthal, Tamor, and Walmsley (1983), Calkins (1983), and Graves (1983). The growing interest in this new process approach does not mean that product-based research should be rejected (Langer, 1984); both approaches together have, in fact, provided answers that neither alone could provide (Schumacher, Klare, Cronin, and Moses, 1984). Fortunately, useful books based on a product approach continue to appear (e.g., Hirsch, 1977), and both approaches can be found in other recent books (e.g., Anderson, Brockmann, and Miller, 1983).

The suggestions in this chapter on writing readably therefore come from research using both product and process approaches. They are based primarily on research at the levels of words, sentences, and coherence and organization; they can be applied in either original writing or in rewriting material to make it more readable. The need for more readable writing may in some cases be obvious as writers edit their own work. In other situations, knowledge of the intended readers' competence or motivation, or the nature of the material, may indicate the need; or, a readability formula score (described in Chapter 7) may do so.

Applying the suggestions in writing versus rewriting is much the same procedure, except that in writing one may 'select' words or sentence structures and in rewriting one usually 'changes' them. Phrasing the suggestions both ways would be clumsy, since this editing process is so similar and so common. Hayes and Flower (1980a) point out that editing appears to take precedence over all other writing processes in the sense that it may interrupt other processes at any time. 'Changes', then, will be used in this chapter; the term is more general than 'selects', and will apply both to writers changing their original writing or editing someone else's.

The development and growing use of sophisticated computer-based editing systems blurs the line between the two processes still further. Early editing programs covered straightforward grammatical features or, at most, customs of language usage. Several recent systems, however, include complex analysis and comparison features useful for readable writing. (Many of the features from Tables 1 and 2 of this chapter appear in programmed form in one or more of the systems below.) Research workers at Bell Laboratories (see Macdonald, Frase, Gingrich, and Keenan, 1982; see also the series of articles by Frase, 1983, Macdonald, 1983, and Gingrich, 1983) developed the most complete and widely used system, the Writer's Workbench. Bell Laboratories franchises its use. Research workers at the US Navy's Training and Evaluation Group (see Kincaid, Aagard, O'Hara, and Cottrell, 1981; see also Kincaid, Braby, and Wulfeck, 1983) developed the Computer Readability Editing System, or CRES. Several large suppliers of technical equipment use this system by arrangement with the US Navy. The Westinghouse Writing Aids System, or WRITEAIDS (see Kniffin, undated), contains some of the same features as the other two, with development still under way. These systems typically provide printouts of their analyses and comparisons for a text; writers (or editors) can then change the copy. Recent work, however, has begun to make some interactive analyses possible at a computer terminal; writers can thus as easily 'select' as 'change' to desirable word and sentence structures as they write.

Maintaining the distinction between 'change' and 'select', then, seems no longer needed for this chapter. Even the distinction between word and sentence changes versus coherence and organization changes appears artificial at times. This division has been kept, however, because the research can best be presented this way. And because writers typically consider organization and coherence earlier in the writing task, suggestions of this sort appear first below.

Coherence and Organization Changes

The term 'coherence', as used in this chapter, refers to what links sentences in a text to each other, while 'organization' refers to the way in which all sentences in the text relate to the abstract structure (the schema or theme). Readers proceeding through a text follow the propositions laid down for them by the writer. If readers must recall what they have read, as noted in the last chapter, organizing relations in terms of cause and effect or contrast appears superior to presenting them as problems and solutions. How can a writer put this to use?

Cause-effect relationships, to take a first case, can be expressed in several different ways. The cause can come first, followed by the effect ('normal order'); or the effect can come first, followed by the cause ('reverse order'). Which comes first makes relatively little difference according to a study by Irwin (1980a) unless the cause-effect relationship is left implicit rather than made explicit. Some highly simplified examples show these relations in the following order: 1. normal-explicit; 2. reverse-explicit; 3. normal-implicit; and 4. reverse-implicit.

1. Because they did not understand their bill, they called the Business Office.

2. They called the Business Office because they did not understand their bill.

3. They did not understand their bill. They called the Business Office.

4. They called the Business Office. They did not understand their bill.

What can this and related studies mean for writers? Readers recall straightforward (explicit) cause-effect relationships better than those which require inferences (implicit). This effect increases for readers who are less skilled or mature (Irwin, 1982), and as writing becomes more complex and involves both order and clarity. In such cases, writers may be tempted to divide a long sentence into two sentences for greater readability. As these studies show, however, such division may have the opposite result unless the cause-effect relationship is rather obvious.

Furthermore, where 'connectives' can be used, they help readers to recall relationships. In addition to cause-effect, conditional ('if-then') and temporal ('first-second', or **when**) relationships can be improved. The following versions of the above sentences express explicit conditional relations (1. and 2.) and temporal relations (3. and 4.), with the connectives included.

1. If they do not understand their bill they should call the Business Office.

2. They should call the Business Office if they do not understand their bill.

3. When they do not understand their bill, they should call the Business Office.

4. They should call the Business Office when they do not understand their bill.

With the explicit connectives removed, and in more complex writing, less skilled readers may make – and remember – incorrect inferences.

Contrast as well as cause-and-effect relationships have proved effective for readers asked to recall information later. How can material be organized to emphasize contrast? Useful answers have begun to come from the research in coherence, on the way sentences (or propositions) are linked to each other. Hobbs (1979) lists three coherence relations: *elaboration, parallel*, and *contrast*. In elaboration, the second item repeats some old information and gives some new information as well. This construction, as in the example below, serves to overcome possible misunderstanding or lack of understanding.

Look in the Yellow Pages. Just look for the heading 'Restaurants' in the Yellow Pages.

A parallel construction presents parts of a sentence that are parallel in meaning in a structure (pattern) that is also parallel. Readers can handle this arrangement with less mental processing, or reinterpretation, as the second example below illustrates.

Jack is a proofreader who is fast, accurate, and has capability.
Jack is a proofreader who is fast, accurate, and capable.

Contrast arrangements have one pair of contrary elements, but the other pair or pairs are similar. Whereas parallel constructions invite readers to generalize, contrast constructions emphasize when readers should not generalize.

You are not likely to reach them at that number, but

you are more likely to reach them there than at the other numbers they gave you.

Other cohesive relationships. A number of other cohesive relationships have been described by Halliday and Hasan (1976). They list the following constructions for linking sentences to each other.

- *referential*, or the use of personals (e.g., you, he, she), demonstratives (e.g., this, that) or comparatives (e.g., another, more, else).
- *substitution*, or the replacement of one word with another in a subsequent use;
- *ellipsis*, or the obvious omission of a repeated concept;
- *conjunction*, or a semantic (meaning) relationship between sentences; and
- *lexical*, or repetition and collocation (the use of words which regularly occur together, such as king and queen, or north and south).

Irwin (1980b) has shown that one version of a passage with twice as many cohesive ties as another can be significantly more readable (comprehensible). The study thus supports Kintsch's view of comprehension, as described in Chapter 5.

Marshall (1979) has summarized research on the relationships between readability and the structure of text (i.e., coherence and organization). The major findings indicate that readers remember:

- main ideas better than details, no matter where the main ideas occur in a piece of writing.
- repeated words better than words used only once, and repeated information better than novel information.
- explicitly related ideas better than unrelated ideas.
- information tied to a reader's prior knowledge better than information that is not.

Marshall concludes that main ideas and higher-level concepts can be used to organize information best when they are familiar and are explicitly stated. This arrangement then, in turn, aids in the understanding of lower-level concepts. For those interested in exploring the research on coherence and organization, Shimmerlik (1978), Marshall and Glock (1978–79), Reder (1980) and Pearson and Camperell (1981), present useful reviews and summaries. The dates of these articles indicate, quite appropriately, a growing area where new findings can be expected to modify the old. This emphasizes, once again, that such information must be considered as suggestions, to be used with discretion, and not rules. This applies to the next sections on words and sentences as well.

Word Changes

Before discussing word changes, the earlier distinction between 'content' words and 'function' words needs emphasizing. Content words are primarily nouns, verbs, adjectives, and adverbs, because they carry most of the **content** of a message; pronouns and numbers are often included also. Function words are most often the remaining categories (articles, prepositions, conjunctions, etc.), because they typically show **functional** relationship or structure. Words can, of course, shift grammatical roles in English usage, so this division is not rigid. Nevertheless, the distinction is necessary because most of the word changes described here apply only to words carrying content. Within this division, most of the research has been done with nouns. Recently, however, the research has been extended to verbs and adjectives, and has included some adverbial forms. Because of the important role of verbs as well as nouns in readable writing, including verbs has been especially valuable.

Six word changes, or variables, are listed briefly below. Specific suggestions for using them in writing or rewriting follow this list. For those interested, Table 1, Some Word Difficulty Variables, summarizes the supporting research results. References given are only a partial list of those available, and are meant to be illustrative. As such, they contain some qualified as well as some clearly positive results.

These word variables tend to be related to each other, i.e., frequently used words are usually shorter than those infrequently used. The variables are not **perfectly** related, however, so each is discussed separately.

1. *Word frequency and familiarity.* Words of high (versus low) frequency and/or familiarity contribute to more readable writing; found for nouns particularly, but also for other content words. Compare *meal* with *repast*, *household* with *menage*, *leave* with *depart*, *count* with *reckon*.

2. *Word length.* Shorter words (versus longer) tend to make writing more readable; generally found for content words, but sometimes also for function words. Examples are *owner* versus *proprietor*, *go* versus *proceed*, *bloody* versus *sanguinary*, *too* versus *additionally*.

3. *Association-value.* Words which call up other words quickly and easily add to readability of writing more than those which do not; studies made with nouns chiefly, but several with adjectives. *Girl* brings *boy* to mind more quickly than *man*, *hand* suggests *foot* sooner than *leg*, and *sleepy* suggests *drowsy* before *heavy*; *love* calls up associations more easily than *amour*, and *law* more quickly than *decree*.

4. *Concreteness – abstractness.* Concrete words, which easily arouse an image in one's mind, contribute more

to readable writing than words which do not (abstract words); studies made with nouns and verbs, primarily. Winston Churchill must have known instinctively about this; he chose *blood, sweat, toil,* and *tears* over something like *bravery, energy,* and *sadness.* Some politicians like to use abstract words like *victory* and *heroism,* whereas their hearers are more likely to visualize and remember *village* and *hospital.* But the difference is easy to miss: *time* is abstract while *timepiece* (and *clock*) are concrete. Adjectives have been scaled for the related quality of vividness. *Savage* is more vivid than *heartless,* for example, and *filthy* than *soiled.*

5. *Active verbs versus nominalizations.* The active verb form tends to make writing more readable than the nominalized form; nominalizations are words (usually verbs) made into noun form. *Consider* may thus become *the consideration of, oppose* become *the opposition to,* or *suppose* become *the supposition that.*

6. *Pronouns and other anaphora.* Anaphora are words, notably pronouns, or phrases which refer back to a previous word or unit of text. Examples of anaphora, besides pronouns such as *he* and *she* or *that* and *which,* are phrases like *the above* or *defined earlier* or *in the third paragraph.* When using anaphora, clarify what they refer to. Research shows that the distance between a pronoun and its referent affects comprehension of both the pronoun and its referent.

Several other word variables might have been added, notably: the absence (versus the presence) of affixed morphemes (prefixes and suffixes); and, use of words of Anglo-Saxon (as opposed to Latin) origin. These variables are highly related to one or more of the others listed, and are not as easy to apply, so they have not been given separate listing.

Using word changes in rewriting. How can the six word variables be put to work by a writer who wishes to use easier (more readable) words in place of harder (less readable)? A suggested series of steps is given below, but use whatever procedure you find most useful. A few words of qualification are needed first, however. To begin, not all potentially hard words should be changed; some cannot be without an undesirable change of meaning. In addition, a good or better substitute word (or short phrase) cannot always be found or be inserted without undesirable sentence changes. Good editorial opinion is essential. Where the following steps do suggest useful substitutions, such word changes can help to make writing more readable.

1. When going through the passage, check the content words likely to be difficult. A good rough index is length in syllables or letters.

2. Avoid changing technical or similar special-meaning terms (if any). Better substitutes cannot usually be found for them. Instead, provide definitions along with the terms if they are unlikely to be familiar to the intended reader (e.g., have not been defined before).

3. Look for several more frequent or familiar substitutes (single words or short phrases) for the difficult content words. Several sources are available.

   a. One's own knowledge can often serve. Frequency 'tagging' appears to be an automatic and, in fact, an essential component in our 'processing' of the world. This is especially the case for words, and can even be found in young children (Hasher and Chromiak, 1977). Studies show that we tend to think of more frequent synonyms for words before we think of less frequent, so our own knowledge can indeed be a valuable resource.

    b. To find substitutes when necessary, use a dictionary specifically designed to give highest-frequency definitions first. Good sources are the *Thorndike-Barnhart Handy Dictionary* (1955), *The American College Dictionary* (Barnhart, 1947), *Dictionary of Modern English Usage* (Fowler, 1974) and *The American Heritage Dictionary if the English Language* (Davies, 1976) in one of its several hardcover or paperback editions. Other interesting but not as readily available sources are Michael West's *The New Method English Dictionary Explaining the Meaning of 24 000 Items Within a Vocabulary of 1490 Words* (1935) or his *A General Service List of English Words* (1953). The latter classifies the commonest 2000 words in terms of the frequency of their different meanings, and in the process provides common synonyms.

    c. A thesaurus, or dictionary of synonyms, provides still more words. *Soule's Dictionary of English Synonyms* (Sheffield, 1959) is an excellent source book and is in paperback. Other possibilities include one of the available books with the words 'Roget' and/or 'thesaurus' in the title. If using such a source, a check on frequency is sometimes desirable. Thorndike and Lorge's *The Teacher's Word Book of 30 000 Words* (1944) is one way to make a check. There have been some questions of the adequacy of its sampling and of the currency of the words. For a more recent count, especially appropriate for adult usage, Kucera and Francis's *Computational Analysis of Present-Day American English* (1967) is preferable. *The American Heritage Word Frequency Book* by Carroll, Davies, and Richman (1971) provides a more recent count for children.

4. From among the several substitutes located, check to see which satisfy the following qualifications:

a. It is highly concrete? Does it describe an object that can be perceived by the senses? Does it refer to a person, place, or thing that can be seen, heard, felt, smelled, or tasted? Does it have a relatively direct reference to objects, to material, or to sources of sensation? If yes on one or more counts, the word is concrete and likely to be more readable than one which does not qualify. Compare, for example, *key* versus *effect*, or *sailor* versus *anyone*. The psychologists Otfried Spreen and Rudolph Schulz (1966) have compiled a list of 329 nouns that vary in concreteness; Allan Paivio, John Yuille, and Stephen Madigan (1968) have provided a list of 925 nouns varying both in concreteness and the closely related quality of imagery. Howard Walker (1970) has developed imagery ratings for 338 nouns. C. Hess Haagen (1949) considers an adjective vivid if it leaves a clear or graphic impression, which appears similar to the definition of concreteness in nouns. He has provided vividness ratings of 400 pairs of common adjectives. Compare, for example, how much more vivid *frantic* is than *confused*, or *putrid* is than *impure*. Michael Toglia and William F. Battig have provided a very complete and recent source of information in their *Handbook of Semantic Word Norms* (1978). It contains concreteness and imagery ratings of 2854 words of all parts of speech.

b. Does it have a high association-value, particularly with another word used in the passage? This can be roughly determined from one's own experience (e.g., *green – grass* and *go – fast* are higher in association-value than *green – house*, or *go – quickly*. These values vary somewhat according to the reader's grade or reading age level. To find a high-associate word for the various grades, a good source

Table 1: *Some Word Difficulty Variables*

Variable	Performance Score(s)	References: Name and Date	Comment
1. Word frequency and familiarity, especially of nouns	Reading efficiency; reader judgements; recall; for nouns, particularly, comprehension	Klare, 1968 (review); Coleman, 1971; Elley, 1969; Glanzer and Bowles, 1976; Gorman, 1961; Thorndike and Garrettson, unpublished; see also Kirkman, 1980 (review)	Words of high (*v* low) frequency of occurrence and familiarity result in: increased recall, reading efficiency (recognition time), and reader preferences. However, frequency of content (*v* function) words, particularly nouns, seems to provide the relationship to comprehension and performance.
2. Word length	Reading speed and fixations; cloze comprehension scores and information gain; in some cases, recognition time may not be affected	Klare, 1968 (review); see also Bormuth, 1966; Coleman and Miller, 1968; and Coleman, 1971; see, however, Richards and Heller, 1976	Review shows use of shorter (*v* longer) words results in faster recognition time and reading speed, fewer fixations; also, shorter words related to higher cloze comprehension scores and information gain.

Variable	Performance Score(s)	References: Name and Date	Comment
3. Association-value	Reading speed, comprehension, and learning	Coleman, 1965; Rosenberg, 1966; Samuels, 1968; see also Paivio, 1969	Use of high (v low) association-value words (particularly nouns and adjectives) results in increased reading speed, comprehension, and learning.
4. Concreteness – abstractness	Recognition and recall memory, judgements of readability, and sentence usage; also, information gain and recognition time	Gorman, 1961; Coleman and Blumenfeld, 1963; Dukes and Bastian, 1966; Thorndike and Garrettson, unpublished; Elley, 1969; Coleman, 1971; Yuille and Paivio, 1969; Montague and Carter, 1973; Richards, 1976	Concrete (v abstract) words result in increased recognition and recall memory and readability judgements, more correct sentence usage, and greater information gain. In some cases, recognition time is speeded up. (Concrete words defined as arousing a sensory image.)

Variable	Performance Score(s)	References: Name and Date	Comment
5. Active verbs versus nominali-zations	Comprehension, cloze and multiple-choice; recall; information gain	Coleman and Blumenfeld, 1963; Coleman, 1964, 1965, 1968; Rohrman, 1968	Sentences using nominalizations more difficult to comprehend and recall than those using active verbs; subject nominalizations recalled better than object nominalizations.
6. Pronouns and other anaphora	Cloze scores; recall	Coleman, 1971; Bormuth, 1966 and 1969; Marshall, 1979	Some evidence that increased use of pronouns, and particularly of all anaphora, relate to difficulty; also, that distance between pronouns and their referents affects comprehension.

of information is David Palermo and James Jenkins' *Word Association Norms, Grade School through College* (1964). Another source of data is Leo Postman and Geoffrey Keppel's *Norms of Word Association* (1970). The 925 nouns of Paivio, Yuille, and Madigan (1968) have also been rated for meaningfulness (i.e., association-value). Compare *arm* versus *forehead* in terms of how many associations each elicits, or *nail* versus *keg*. The association value of 400 pairs of common adjectives may be found in the list prepared by Haagen (1949). Some examples are: *frigid* is rated as much more closely associated to *icy* than to *gelid*, and *liquid* to *fluid* more than to *limpid*. The Toglia and Battig book mentioned above also provides ratings for meaningfulness and number of attributes for all categories of words.

c. Is it a word whose common (rather than uncommon) meaning is called for? Two things help: the human tendency to think first of common rather than uncommon meanings, and the context (see item 8. below). For example, *run* is said to have at least 97 different dictionary meanings, ranging from *go faster than walking* to *manage a business*, from a *run of one mile* to a *run on the bank*, from *run up* to *run down*. You can easily think of the most common ones, but the less common come only with difficulty. The same is true for a reader, unless the context is especially clear. If you want help, the *Thorndike-Barnhart Handy Dictionary*, the *American College Dictionary*, and *The American Heritage Dictionary of the English Language* list definitions roughly in order of their frequency of use. Edgar Dale and Joseph O'Rourke's *The Living Word Vocabulary* (1981) gives even more precise information by indicating grade levels (from 4th grade through college graduate) when the various meanings of a word are known.

d. To show how high-frequency nouns that are concrete and have high association-value differ from those that are less concrete and have lower association-value, consider the two groups: (1) *bread, sheep, teeth, breakfast, diamond;* (2) *fate, fault, custom, presence, circumstance.*

e. If none of the above characteristics (concreteness, association-value, common meaning, or frequency) can be applied, choose the shorter word if it fits as well. There is a tendency for length to be related to the above variables, anyway.

5. Change nominalizations, where possible, to their active verb counterparts. An example would be the change from *Noah's construction of the ark* to *Noah constructed the ark* or, still better, *Noah built the ark.* Others would be *Marilyn's applications of the suntan oil* to *Marilyn applied the suntan oil* and *John's derivation of the formula* to *John derived the formula.*

6. Review the anaphoric constructions to see if they should be expanded or can be moved closer to their referents. Where a pronoun is used, substitute its noun referent if you feel the reader needs help. Look for phrases or clauses such as *The previous example* or *The above paragraph showed why* and add qualifiers if necessary, such as *The previous example of concrete words* or *The above paragraph on association-value showed why.*

7. Choose adverbs carefully to show the desired degree of intensity. A study by Norman Cliff (1959) indicates that readers are highly consistent in saying how much a particular adverb (e.g., *slightly* versus *very*) multiplies the intensity of adjectives (such as *evil* or *charming*). The typical rank from low intensity to high is:

(1) **slightly** modifying the adjective = least multiplication

(2) **somewhat**

(3) **rather**

(4) **pretty**

(5) **quite**

(6) **decidedly**

(7) **unusually**

(8) **very**

(9) **extremely** modifying the adjective = greatest multiplication

The unmodified adjective usually was found at about the rank of *quite* or *decidedly*.

8. Keep in mind that when a reader encounters a difficult word, the four or so words on each side of it are critical. A reader may be trying to find a substitute for the word, determine which of the word's several meanings is intended, or guess the word (when a blank has replaced it). Note how the meaning of **type** is determined by the words surrounding it in the following four sentence fragments: . . . **is a face of the type that he can show** . . . ; . . . **he shows it is type of a face that can** . . . ; . . . **shows that he can type a face of the** . . . ; . . . **shows that he can type it if the faces of** . . . . It is therefore important that the four or so words in the neighbourhood of a critical term be understandable and helpful.

9. Terms or expressions known to be highly familiar to an intended reading audience are exceptions to the above steps; they should be used, of course, even though they are relatively unfamiliar to others. For example, some terms may not meet the qualifications described and yet be clear to readers (or better yet, hearers) in a given cultural, geographic, or racial

group. When examples or analogies are used, they can be more effective if they are situations familiar to intended readers and related to their interests.

10. Avoid unnecessary words. This suggestion, commonly given in books on writing, is particularly important. 'Brevity consistent with clarity' contributes to reading speed (efficiency) and to depth of reading. One writer put it well in saying, 'With a little more time I could have made that message clearer by **shortening** it.'

11. To summarize briefly, writers can usually find words that need changing by keeping these questions in mind when re-reading what they have written:

   a. *Is the word long?*
   b. *Will intended readers know the word?*
   c. *Is the word necessary?*

Word changes alone are clearly not enough in most revisions. To be sure, they cannot **even be made** alone in all cases (e.g., when changing nominalizations to active verbs). Changing phrases, clauses, or other sentence structures is often also necessary. The next section deals with changes within sentences.

Sentence Changes

The sentence changes described below involve six variables. Specific suggestions for using them in writing or rewriting follow this list, along with further definition of the variables. For those interested, Table 2, Some Sentence Difficulty Variables, summarizes the supporting research results. As with the earlier word changes, the references are only a partial list of those available, and are meant to be illustrative. As such, they contain some qualified as well as some clearly positive results.

1. *Length.* Shortened sentences and clauses (to be described later) contribute to more readable writing.

2. *Statement v question constructions.* Statements tend to produce better recall than questions in typical text.

3. *Affirmative v negative statements.* Positive constructions are likely to be verified more quickly and with fewer errors than negative (i.e., those including negative words).

4. *Active v passive statements.* The active voice leads to easier recall and verification than the passive.

5. *Self-embedded v non-embedded constructions.* Self-embedded statements (i.e., those with repeated parts within parallel elements in the sentence, illustrated on page 109) greatly reduce readability compared to non-embedded alternatives.

6. *Depth of words in sentences.* Greater word depths (i.e., words with more 'commitments' the reader must store while reading, as illustrated on page 109) make writing less readable.

A few preliminary words may be helpful before suggesting how to use the above variables. Many of the changes described below come from studies using transformational grammar. They are, thus, subject to modification as newer data become available. In addition, the studies have sometimes been done only with single sentences, since experimental work with passage-length materials is difficult. Therefore, the suggested changes do not have the status of rules, and should not be made mechanically.

First, not all potentially difficult sentences should be

Table 2: *Some Sentence Difficulty Variables*

Variables	Performance Score(s)	References: Name and Date	Comment
1. Length (including clause length)	Comprehension, cloze scores, and time	Coleman, 1962, 1965, and 1971; Gough, 1966; Stoodt, 1972; see also Kirkman 1980 (review)	Certain changes in sentence length are effective (e.g., dividing sentences joined by conjunctions such as **but, for, because,** etc.), but others have little effect; clause length as important as sentence length, and changing clauses to full sentences effective.
2. Statements versus questions	Recall	Mehler, 1963; Savin and Perchonock, 1965	Recall better for statements than questions (in either active or passive form).
3. Affirmative versus negative statements	Verification (by observation) of truth or falsity	Gough, 1965 and 1966; Slobin, 1966	Negative statements required more time or caused more errors in verification (using a true-false test) than affirmative statements.

Variables	Performance Score(s)	References: Name and Date	Comment
4. Active versus passive statements	Verification; recall	Mehler, 1963; Coleman, 1965; Gough, 1965 and 1966; Prentice, 1966; Slobin, 1968; Blount and Johnson, 1973; Ramsey, 1980	Active statements verified more readily and retained better than passive statements (this appears more clearly for reversible than non-reversible statements, for full than truncated passives, and for sentences where events are presented in the correct temporal order).
5. Embeddedness	Cloze scores and paraphrases for comprehension	Coleman, 1965; Schlesinger, 1968; Blumenthal, 1966; Hakes and Cairns, 1970; Hamilton and Deese, 1971	Self-embedded sentences cause the reader difficulty; inserting relative pronouns helps, but a right-branching construction is preferred.
6. Depth	Cloze scores; recall	Bormuth, 1964 and 1966; Martin and Roberts, 1966; Rohrman, 1968; Herriott, 1968; MacGinttie and Tretiak, 1971; Wearing, 1972	Sentences with low mean word depth comprehended and recalled better than those with high word depth (but see Rohrman for a criticism).

changed. Sentence variety adds to the pleasure of reading, and is probably desirable even in the simplest writing. We need information on when (in terms of age or reading skill) various constructions can be readily understood by readers, and such work is now moving steadily ahead.

Second, sentence changes are often most effective when potential word changes are considered at the same time; in fact, studies indicate that changing only one or the other in an entire passage may not make it much more readable than it was. Both kinds of changes should be made together when this can be done. And just as mentioned for word changes, good editorial opinion is essential.

Making all of the changes suggested at all times, however, is seldom possible; where possible, seldom desirable; where desirable, seldom necessary. Where one or more changes can be made, however, consider doing this since it can often make writing more readable. As one writer points out, the changes a good editor makes intuitively are frequently the kinds of transformations suggested by the experimental research.

Using sentence changes in rewriting. The suggested sentence changes are described in the series of steps below. Consider them with the above cautions in mind.

1. Look at the sentences in the passage, with particular attention to the longer sentences. Not all long sentences are difficult to understand; but reviewing is useful because length and difficulty tend to be related. Several kinds of changes can often be made in long sentences.

   a. Look for compound or compound-complex sentences containing conjunctions such as **but**, **for**, or **because**. Dividing such sentences into two by changing clauses to full sentences can make writing more readable. Dividing sentences joined by **and** has much less effect.

b. Sentences may be long because they are composed of one long clause or of two, or more, relatively long clauses. As it happens, clause length is important to comprehension apart from sentence length as a whole, so reducing clause length can be helpful.

c. Long sentences usually contain complex structures, but complexity may not always be reflected in length. This is particularly true for *transformations*. Briefly, transformations involve rules for rewriting sentences and analysing them into grammatically related parts. Examples will follow, but if you want a more complete description, a good reference is Emmon Bach's *An Introduction to Transformational Grammars* (1964).

2. Change questions to statements, where this is possible and a high degree of text simplification is desired. A possible change would be to transform **Could the other driver have been blinded by the sun?** to **The other driver could have been blinded by the sun.** Do not interpret this suggestion to mean that all questions should be avoided. Questions play a natural and necessary role, of course, in requesting information. Furthermore, they can be effective in the learning and retention of instructional material (see Rothkoff, 1977, for a review). In general text, however, changing from question to statement form may help readers in the later recall of information.

3. Change negative to affirmative statements where possible and acceptable. For example, **The man who designed the Brooklyn Bridge is not alive** can be changed to **The man who designed the Brooklyn Bridge is dead**. Relating such a change to sentence

complexity is easier when a more complex sentence is involved. **This is George Washington's Mount Vernon mansion**, or even **Is this George Washington's Mount Vernon mansion?**, may both be preferable to **Is this not George Washington's Mount Vernon mansion?**

4. Change passive to active sentences where possible and acceptable, particularly where the statements are 'reversible'. An example of a reversible sentence is **Jack jumped over Jill**. Jill could possibly jump over Jack, and this must presumably be kept in mind. In the non-reversible statement, **Jack jumped over the candlestick**, the unlikelihood of the candlestick jumping over Jack simplifies the matter for the reader.

   When the passive form is used for a particular kind of emphasis, a change to active form may be undesirable. This is particualrly important if you reverse the order in which events actually occurred when changing from passive to active form. For example, the kind of change from **The raindance was performed before they planted the corn** to **They planted the corn after performing the raindance** was found to cause a loss or error in long-term memory.

   Also, while full passives are clearly harder than active forms, truncated (shortened) passives are little, if any, harder. Examples of full and truncated passives are: **They were taken to their seats by the usher** versus **They were taken to their seats**. Even in such cases there is some superiority of active over passive form, however. Active forms show the actor-action relationship more clearly, and (especially in documents) assign responsibility more clearly. The passive form has therefore sometimes been called 'the evasive passive'.

5. Change (or avoid) self-embedded sentences where

possible, since even skilled readers tend to misinterpret them. An example would be **The car the man the dog bit drove crashed**. If such a sentence *is* needed, inserting relative pronouns aids comprehension. The sentence might then become **The car which the man that the dog bit drove crashed**. Changing to a 'right-recursive' or 'right-branching' form, such as **This is the dog that bit the man that drove the car that crashed**, is still better. Both right-recursive and left-recursive sentences, such as **Lincoln's doctor's wife's dog bit the driver of the car and it crashed**, are easier to understand then self-embedded sentences. Constructions that contain more than two self-embedded clauses are uncommon in English, and are almost incomprehensible even to skilled readers. Right-branching constructions of a simple sort using relative clauses are, however, more common and much easier to understand.

6. Change constructions that are high in word depth to ones that are low (when possible). Word depth, as indicated earlier, refers to the 'commitments' words have as parts of sentences; readers must presumably remember these commitments as they read through them. Sentences with many modifiers, particularly complex ones, contain words with high word depth. An example is **He, whom we saw in New York City, which we visited shortly before Christmas despite the bitter weather, is now in Europe**. Victor Yngve (1960) devised a scheme to assign depth numbers to words. The procedure is complex, however, and need not be given here. It is enough to say that this sentence, as others like it, can easily be changed to a more readable form: **He is now in Europe. We saw him shortly before Christmas in New York City, in spite of the bitter weather**.

7. The above changes suggest that the easiest sentence to understand is a Simple, Active, Affirmative, Declarative (SAAD) sentence – just as some teachers of writing have said. The changes may also suggest that the more 'transformations' from the SAAD structure, the less understandable the sentence becomes. This is not necessarily **always** the case. There seems little doubt, however, that high word depth and self-embedded structures are among the major contributors to difficulty of understanding, at least as far as raters are concerned.

   Even such complicated constructions may contribute to difficulty chiefly because we see them so little rather than because of innate complexity. Frieda Goldman-Eisler and Michele Cohen (1970) have pointed out that SAAD sentences make up 80-90 per cent of the prepared and spontaneous **speech** of such varied groups as eminent lecturers and schizophrenics. Negative and passive constructions make up only seven to ten per cent of such speech, and passive-negative constructions (and self-embedded structures) are practically non-events. Though such constructions appear more in writing than in speech, they are still relatively rare. And there is now some evidence that practice on complex self-embedded structures helps readers to understand new ones.

   Whatever the reason for their effectiveness, their simplicity of grammatical structure or their frequency, SAAD sentences are usually very clear. Difficulty of a passage becomes a matter of how many other, more complicated structures are included among them. Variety is desirable, but too many complications are not.

8. To summarize sentence changes briefly, a writer can help to locate sentences which need changing by keep-

ing three questions in mind:

a. Is the sentence long and complex?
b. Will intended readers understand the sentence?
c. Is the variety needed, or should I simplify the sentence?

Implications for Writers

In summary, readable prose can be described in the following research-based terms.

- **Coherent or cohesive.** The sentences are linked to each other so readers going from one to another readily follow the propositions they contain.
- **Well-organized.** All sentences relate logically to a central theme (or themes, in a longer piece), so readers clearly discern the main idea (or ideas) from the supporting ideas.
- **Familiar in wording.** Content words tend, where appropriate, to be short, frequent, concrete, and high in association-value; the text is high in active verb and low in anaphoric constructions.
- **Well-structured.** Sentences tend, where appropriate, to be short, active, affirmative, and declarative (SAAD); the text avoids high word depth and self-embedding.

To promote efficient reading, writers need to aim for material adjusted to intended readers' skill and motivation levels. Such writing appears neither so hard nor so easy that it turns readers to other activities. The last chapter (7) describes ways to estimate roughly (but quickly) whether a desirable match between writing and reader exists.

An example of not-so-readable text is the following: **Is this not the malt the rodent the feline the canine aggravated slaughtered consumed that was contained in the residential construction of Jack's?** The sentence is a nursery rhyme made unfit for the nursery but kept grammatically correct. It can be made fit again for even an unskilled reader by changing the words and sentence constructions along the lines suggested above. Here is a series of illustrative steps.

1. **Word changes** (note that many of these changes could have been made on more than one of the bases given earlier).

   a. abstract to concrete: change *rodent* to *rat, feline* to *cat*, and *canine* to *dog*.

   b. low to high association-value: change *feline* to *cat* and *canine* to *dog*.

   c. low frequency/familiarity to high frequency/ familiarity: change *consumed* to *ate, aggravated* to *teased, slaughtered* to *killed*.

   d. long to short: change *aggravated* to *teased* and *slaughtered* to *killed*.

   e. nominalization to active verb form: change *residential construction of Jack's* to *house that Jack built*.

   f.   result of word changes: *Is this not the malt the rat the cat the dog teased killed ate that was contained in the house that Jack built?*

2. **Sentence changes** (note that the changes may be interrelated and that the changed sentences are abbreviated for convenience).

   a. negative to affirmative form: *Is this not the malt . . . Jack built?* to *Is this the malt . . . Jack built?*

   b. interrogative to declarative form: *Is this the malt . . . Jack built?* to *This is the malt . . . Jack built.*

c. passive to active form: *This is the malt . . . was contained in the house that Jack built* to *This is the malt . . . lay in the house that Jack built.*

d. self-embedded without relative pronouns to self-embedded with relative pronouns: *This is the malt the rat the cat the dog teased killed ate . . . Jack built* to *This is the malt that the rat that the cat that the dog teased killed ate . . . Jack built.*

e. self-embedded to right-branching form: *This is the dog that teased the cat that killed the rat that ate the malt that lay in the house that Jack built.*

f. reduced to simplest possible form, if desired: *Jack built a house. Some malt lay in the house. A rat ate the malt. A cat killed the rat. A dog teased the cat.*

Few, if any, sentences you will encounter in English will have as many different denominations of complications as this, although some (like the one you are reading!!) will certainly have phrases that increase word depth or connectives (like **although**) that need to be handled more appropriately, or just plain long words (like **encounter**) or sentence lengths that need alteration. Many words and sentences **can** be changed to make them more readable. This does not mean that we would want to go as far as step *f*; we would do so only if we wanted to reach beginning readers.

Chapter 7

The Readability Level of Written Material

Chapter 1 pointed to two problems in readable writing: prediction and production. **Predicting** readability, though not easy to do well, was said to be relatively simple compared to **producing** readable writing. The two processes are actually quite different. Chapter 7 will focus on prediction, as Chapters 5 and 6 did on production.

Writers, particularly those in education and the mass media, have for a long time faced the problem of judging the level of readability of a piece of writing. Educators know that writing will fail to instruct when it is too hard or too easy for intended readers. Also, writing that is not acceptable to readers of the mass media will turn them away rather than inform them.

Judging Readability

How can writers judge whether their writing is at an appropriate level? A number of methods can be used, varying in ease and in accuracy. The first and most common method is to guess. How good a writer's estimate will be depends heavily upon experience and upon feedback. Unfortunately, writers do not often get direct and immediate feedback as speakers do; writing is a much more remote or detached medium. (Personal letters are, of course, an obvious exception.) Writers often have a human tendency not to see the difficulties in their own writing. If, in addition, they are experts in their field and their readers are novices, the problem is increased. At any rate, writers are usually less accurate in judging the difficulty of their own writing than that of others, usually believing it to be easier to read than it turns out to be.

This suggests a second method of judging the difficulty of writing: asking others to help. This is a good procedure, since groups of about 20 or more judges can reliably rank pieces of writing in order of their difficulty (Harrison, 1980). There are two problems with this method, however. First, you have to find enough co-operative judges. Second, you have to be satisfied with relative judgements – which of several pieces of writing is more or less readable compared to the others. You cannot get a reliable estimate of the difficulty of a single piece of writing, since benchmarks for comparison are lacking. Yet as a writer that is what you most often need.

This in turn suggests another method: testing a piece of writing on a sample of potential readers. Testing is the most accurate method of all when done well, but the most laborious. Few writers can do this, even though it comes closest to giving a specific level of difficulty.

The method of judging readability that has grown recently involves a readability formula, as noted in Chapter 1. Formulas are developed by studying the relationship of various style variables in passages of text, such as percentage of abstract nouns, percentage of infrequent words, etc., to scores of readers on comprehension tests on the passages. When high relationships are found, these variables are combined statistically into a formula that yields a score indicative of the difficulty of a particular passage. Literally hundreds of such potential index variables have been studied. One researcher studied well over 150 before settling on those to use in his formulas.

Studies have shown that proper counts of two simple variables like word length in syllables and sentence length in words (from among the hundreds studied) can do a pretty good job of prediction. They cannot be improved upon very much, either by using more – or more complex – variables. In fact, using many variables not only makes prediction harder but may actually also make it less reliable.

Production, as we saw in Chapter 6, is another matter. Mechanically changing word length and sentence length when writing or rewriting does not make material correspondingly easier; here, more – and more complex – changes **are** needed. Only for prediction are two simple variables sufficient.

One reason for this predictiveness is that elements of language are often highly inter-related. For example, it has been shown that word depths per sentence, a very complicated measure, is highly related to the very simple measure of number of words per sentence in a large sample of writings. Similarly, number of letters per 100 words is almost perfectly related to number of morphemes per 100 words, again a more complicated measure. It is not necessary or desirable for **predictors** to use a complex element when a simple one will do. **Producers** of readable writing, on the other hand, are often **hampered** by the fact that language elements are inter-related. When they change one variable, others often change also and they cannot tell what has (or has not) been effective. Writing readably is therefore much more difficult to do well than is **predicting** when writing will be readable.

The greater ease of predicting than of producing

readable material should not imply that readability formulas are perfect predictors. For one thing, all such formulas to date use only **style** variables. Other variables, such as the content or topic itself, the interest-value of the content, differences in format, various organizational arrangements, etc., are also important. Formula developers do not deny this; they simply know of no objective way to include them in a formula. A number of attempts have been made to include such variables in a checklist (e.g., Irwin and Davis, 1980), but checklists have never caught on because of their subjectivity and the effort required to use them.

Despite this obvious lack, many formulas have been found to do a good job of predicting difficulty. Though not perfect predictors, they clearly do better than individual judges or, sometimes, even groups of judges.

Choosing and Using a Readability Formula

Chapter 1 pointed out that well over 200 such formulas exist. Why are there so many? Some were designed for children's material, some for adult material. Or they were developed for Spanish or German or Hebrew as well as (in most cases) for English. Or they were planned for application to tests, to military material, or to mathematical text. But even among those for adult material in English, there is a great variety. Some are too simple to give reliable results and some too complex to give reliable results. Some are designed for research, but are too cumbersome for practical application; among them are some for computer application. Still others, clearly, were developed to gain PhD degrees for their authors.

A recent review (Klare, 1984) covers and analyses the extensive work in formula development. But how can one choose among so many formulas when a relatively simple but sufficiently reliable measure is needed?

Several formulas fill this need very nicely. Two developed in 1948, Rudolf Flesch's 'Reading Ease' formula and that developed by Edgar Dale and Jeanne Chall, are still useful for this purpose (the latter is soon to appear in a revised version). Among the measures developed more recently, Len Mugford's formula (1970) is frequently used in the UK, and Edward Fry's Readability Graph (1977) is used extensively in both the US and the UK (where it appeared in its first version; Fry, 1963). Certain other more complex formulas developed recently appear to be more accurate than these, but the differences are typically small when they are tested under similar conditions. Furthermore, even the best of formulas under the best of conditions are not perfect predictors. They give quick, easy estimates of reading difficulty, but certainly not highly accurate measures. In addition, the graded levels of difficulty they provide may be surpassed by highly motivated or informed readers – or be underestimates for poorly motivated or informed ones, to mention two of several limitations. A new approach by the College Board (College Entrance Examination Board, 1980) attempts to avoid certain of the limitations of typical readability formulas, but individual users would find the method too complex to apply themselves.

The Fry Readability Graph is the only one described here – for several reasons. It is easy to apply, very widely used, and available for reproduction because there are no copyright restrictions. In addition, the Fry Graph yields very nearly the same results as the other two formulas mentioned, corresponding particularly closely to the Flesch Reading Ease formula. The Fry Graph and directons for using it, from a 1977 article, appear in Figure 2.

Note that the graph provides readability estimates in terms of approximate reading grade levels. For reading age levels, merely add five to the grade levels, as noted in Chapter 1. The first direction under the graph, which

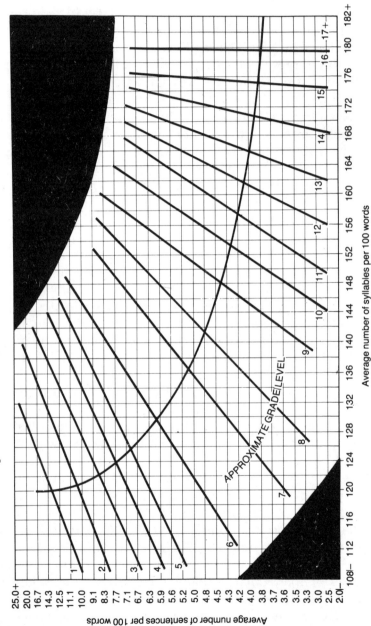

Figure 2 Graph for Estimating Readability – Extended; by Edward Fry, Rutgers University Reading Center, New Brunswick, New Jersey 08904

Expanded Directions for Working Readability Graph

1. Randomly select three (3) sample passages and count out exactly 100 words each, beginning with the beginning of a sentence. Do count proper nouns, initializations, and numerals.
2. Count the number of sentences in the hundred words, estimating length of the fraction of the last sentence to the nearest one-tenth.
3. Count the total number of syllables in the 100-word passage. If you don't have a hand counter available, an easy way is simply to put a mark above every syllable over one in each word, then when you get to the end of the passage, count the number of marks and add 100. Small calculators can also be used as counters by pushing numeral 1, then push the + sign for each word or syllable when counting.
4. Enter graph with *average* sentence length and *average* number of syllables; plot dot where the two lines intersect. Area where dot is plotted will give you the approximate grade level.
5. If a great deal of variability is found in syllable count or sentence count, putting more samples into the average is desirable.
6. A word is defined as a group of symbols with a space on either side; thus, *Joe, IRA, 1945*, and & are each one word.
7. A syllable is defined as a phonetic syllable. Generally, there are as many syllables as vowel sounds. For example, *stopped* is one syllable and *wanted* is two syllables. When counting syllables for numerals and initializations, count one syllable for each symbol. For example, *1945* is four syllables, *IRA* is three syllables, and & is one syllable.

Note: This 'extended graph' does not outmode or render the earlier (1968) version inoperative or inaccurate; it is an extension. (REPRODUCTION PERMITTED – NO COPYRIGHT) suggests taking only three samples, also needs a few words of explanation. Three 100-word samples seem appropriate for relatively short selections, such as chapter-length material, a long memorandum, or a brief lesson, where variability is unlikely to be great. For material of book length, 30 or even more randomly chosen samples may be needed, because variability is more likely to be great (Fitzgerald, 1980, 1981). When analysing multiple-author material, selecting a sample from each writer's contribution helps to check on how much the readability level varies.

If you have a large amount of material to analyse, you might want to consider using a computerized version of one of the formulas. You can do this yourself if you have a home computer that will run one of a number of available programs. Harrison (1980), for example, published a complete listing of a FORTRAN program that will yield Flesch 'Reading Ease' and Mugford readability values as well as Fry Graph coordinates. As another example, Schuyler (1982) published a complete listing of a program in Applesoft BASIC for Apple II computers which will yield readability values for eight formulas, including the Flesch 'Reading Ease', Dale-Chall, and Fry. In the case of the latter, it will provide the graph itself, as well as a composite graph of the values from all of the formulas. Mason, Blanchard, and Daniel (1983) provide references to other programs which you can purchase. They also list addresses for companies that do computer analyses for a fee. Note, however, that unless you have a rather large amount to analyse, a hand analysis can be simpler, quicker, and cheaper if you use the Fry Graph.

Now how should a formula be used? To begin, apply it to a piece of writing to see if the writing is likely to be appropriate to your readers' levels of reading competence and motivation. If it is, you may want to stop there (remembering, however, that even competent and motivated readers welcome a somewhat easier reading task). If your writing appears too difficult for your readers, or if you want to help them read more efficiently, you will need to rewrite. The next step is crucial: do not 'write to formula'. Specifically, do not rewrite merely to make readability formula scores better. It does not work out well, even though the scores make it seem so. Not only will the writing seem mechanical if you chop sentences and make arbitrary word changes, it may also be ineffective in changing reader performance.

Formulas are for **rating**, not for **writing**. Since the variables in the formula were selected only as indices of difficulty (as described in Chapter 1), changing them does not necessarily cause the difficulty of the writing to change accordingly. What you frequently get when you make such changes is an artificially altered readability score, one that is not reflected in increased comprehension by readers. The changes needed in rewriting are more subtle and complex than a formula can suggest, as Chapter 6 indicated. Yet, because of time and cost limitations, the temptation to write to fit a formula is often great and must be consciously avoided (Redish, 1980).

Once your material has been rewritten, **then** apply the formula again. If the material now appears to be appropriate, fine. If not, rewrite again and re-apply the formula.

In this business of checking readability, rewriting, checking again, then rewriting again, seems time-consuming or difficult – it is, at first. After some experience, however, you usually get a feel for the appropriate level for a given body of readers, and the process becomes much faster and easier. Readers are likely to be turned off by writing that seems unnecessarily difficult. Your extra time will not only save time for them, perhaps even thousands of hours; it will also encourage them to read more of what you have written. And that is what readable writing is all about.

References

American College Testing Program. No final answer yet on questions about test score decline. *ACTivity*, *17*, May, 4–5 (1979).

Anderson, P. V., Brockmann, R. J., and Miller, C. R. (Eds.), *New essays in technical and scientific communication: Research, theory, practice*. Farmingdale, N. Y.: Baywood (1983).

Anderson, R. C., and Pearson, P. D. A schema-theoretic view of basic processes in reading comprehension. In P. D. Pearson (Ed.), *Handbook of reading research*. New York: Longman (1984).

Anderson, R. C., and Pichert, J. W. Recall of previously unrecallable information following a shift in perspective. *Journal of Verbal Learning and Verbal Behavior*, *17*, 1–12 (1978).

Anderson, R. C., Spiro, R. J., and Montague, W. E. (Eds.), *Schooling and the acquisition of knowledge*. Hillsdale, N. J.: Erlbaum (1977).

Atlas, M. A. Addressing an audience: A study of expert-novice differences in writing. Technical Report No. 3, Document Design Project. Pittsburgh, Pennsylvania: Carnegie-Mellon University (1979).

Bach, E. *An introduction to transformational grammars*. New York: Holt, Rinehart, and Winston (1964).

Barnhart, C. L. (Ed.) *The American college dictionary*. New York: Harper and Brothers (1947).

Bendick, M., Jr., and Cantu, M. G. The literacy of welfare clients. Washington, DC: The Urban Institute. (Reprinted from *Social Science Review*, 1978, *52*.) (1978).

Berkeley, E. C. Computer-assisted explanation. *Computers and Automation*, *16*, 32–37 (1967).

Blount, H. P., and Johnson, R. E. Grammatical structures and the recall of sentences in prose. *American educational Research Journal*, *10*, 163–8 (1973).

Blumenthal, A. L. Observations with self-embedded sentences. *Psychonomic Science*, *6*, 453–4 (1966).

Bormuth, J. R. Mean word depth as a predictor of comprehension difficulty. *California Journal of Educational Research*, *25*, 226–31 (1964).

Bormuth, J. R. Readability: A new approach. *Reading Research Quarterly*, *1*, 79–132 (1966).

Bormuth, J. R. Development of readability analyses. Final Report, Project No. 7-0052, Contract No. OEC-3-7-070052-0326. Bureau of Research, US Office of Education (1969).

Bransford, J. D., and Franks, J. J. The abstraction of linguistic ideas. *Cognitive Psychology*, *3*, 331–50 (1971).

Bransford, J. D., and Johnson, M. K. Consideration of some problems of comprehension. *Journal of Verbal Learning and Verbal Behavior*, *11*, 717–26 (1972).

Bransford, J. D., and McCarrell, N. S. A sketch of a cognitive approach to comprehension: Some thoughts about understanding what it means to comprehend. In W. B. Weimer and D. S. Palermo (Eds.), *Cognition and the symbolic processes*. Hillsdale, N. J.: Erlbaum (1974).

Britons take aim at gibberish. New York Times, Sunday, 26 December (1982).

Britton, B. K., Westbrook, R. D., and Holdredge, T. S. Reading and cognitive capacity usage. *Journal of Experimental Psychology: Human Learning and Memory*, *4*, 582–91 (1978).

Britton, J., Burgess, T., Martin, N., McLeod, A., and Rosen, H. *The development of writing abilities (11–18)*. Macmillan (1975).

Calkins, L. M. *Lessons from a child: On the teaching and learning of writing*. Heinemann (1983).

Carpenter, P. A., and Just, M. A. Cognitive processes in

reading: Models based on readers' eye fixations. In A. M. Lesgold and C. A. Perfetti (Eds.), *Interactive processes in reading*. Hillsdale, New Jersey: Erlbaum (1981).

Carroll, J. B. The nature of the reading process. In H. Singer and R. B. Ruddell (Eds.), *Theoretical models and processes of reading*. Newark, Delaware: International Reading Association (1970).

Carroll, J. B., Davies, P., and Richman, B. *The American heritage word frequency book*. Boston: Houghton Mifflin (1971).

Carter, J. Executive order 12044: Improving government regulations. Washington, DC: Office of the White house, 23 March, 1978.

Cliff, N. Adverbs as multipliers. *Psychological Review, 66*, 27–44 (1959).

Coleman, E. B. Improving comprehensibility by shortening sentences. *Journal of Applied Psychology, 46*, 131–4 (1962).

Coleman, E. B. The comprehensibility of several grammatical transformations. *Journal of Applied Psychology, 48*, 186–90 (1964).

Coleman, E. B. Learning of prose written in four grammatical transformations. *Journal of Applied Psychology, 49*, 332–41 (1965).

Coleman, E. B. Experimental studies of readability. In J. R. Bormuth (Ed.), *Readability in 1968*. Champaign, Illinois: National Council of Teachers of English (1968).

Coleman, E. B. Developing a technology of written instruction: Some determiners of the complexity of prose. In E. Z. Rothkopf and P. E. Johnson (Eds.), *Verbal learning research and the technology of written instruction*. New York: Teachers College Press, Columbia University (1971).

Coleman, E. B., and Blumenfeld, P. J. Cloze scores of nominalizations and their grammatical transformations using active verbs. *Psychological Reports, 13*, 651–4 (1963).

Coleman, E. B., and Miller, G. R. A measure of information gained during prose learning. *Reading Research Quarterly, 3*, 369–86 (1968).

College Entrance Examination Board. *Users manual, Degrees of Reading Power*. New York: DRP Services, The College Board (1980).

Dale, E., and Chall, J. S. A formula for predicting readability: Instructions, *Educational Research Bulletin*, 27, 37–54 (1948).

Dale, E., and O'Rourke, J. *The living word vocabulary*. Chicago: World Book-Childcraft International (1981).

Davies, P. (Ed.) *The American heritage dictionary of the English language*. New York: Dell (1976).

Department of Education and Science. *A language for life*. Her Majesty's Stationery Office (1975).

Duffy, T. M. Literacy research in the Navy. In T. G. Sticht and D. W. Zapf (Eds.), Reading and readability research in the Armed Services. HumRRO RF-WO-CA-76-4. Alexandria, Virginia: Human Resources Research Organization (1976).

Dukes, W. F., and Bastian, J. Recall of abstract and concrete words equated for meaningfulness. *Journal of Verbal Learning and Verbal Behavior*, 5, 455–8 (1966).

Education Reporter. Rules for writing. *The News Letter* (Ohio State University College of Education), 35, April 1, (1970).

Elley, W. B. The assessment of readability by noun frequency counts. *Reading Research Quarterly*, 4, 411–27 (1969).

Ellis, H. C., and Hunt, R. R. *Fundamentals of human memory and cognition* (Third Edition). Dubuque, Iowa: William C. Brown (1983).

Emig, J. *The composing processes of twelfth graders*. Champaign, Illinois: National Council for Teachers of English. (Research Report No. 13.) (1971).

Entin, E. B. and Klare, G. R. Relationships of measures of interest, prior knowledge, and readability to comprehension of expository passages. In B. Hutson (Ed.), *Advances in reading/language research, Volume III*. Greenwich, Conn.: JAI Press (1985).

FAA Academy. Rules governing the use of aeronautical apparatus. First known airplane flight manual: Instructions issued with the Glen Curtis 'Pusher'. Reissued by the Engineering and Manufacturing Branch, FAA Academy (Washington, DC). Original dated 1911.

Field, R. F. *The art of plain talk*. London and New York: Collier-Macmillan (1962).

Fitzgerald, G. G. Reliability of the Fry sampling procedure. *Reading Research Quarterly*, 15, 489–503 (1980).

Fitzgerald, G. G. How many samples give a good readability estimate? – The Fry Graph. *Journal of Reading*, *24*, 404–10 (1981).

Flavell, J. H. *The development of inferences about others*. In T. Mischel (Ed.), *Understanding other persons*. Basil Blackwell (1974).

Flesch, R. F. A new readability yardstick. *Journal of Applied Psychology*, *32*, 221–33 (1948).

Flesch, R. F. *The art of plain talk*. New York: Harper and Brothers (1946).

Flesch, R. F. *The art of readable writing*. New York: Harper and Brothers (1949).

Flesch, R. F. *How to test readability*. New York: Harper and Brothers (1950).

Flower, L. S., and Hayes, J. R. Cognition of discovery: Defining a rhetorical problem. *College Composition and Communication*, *31*, 21–32 (1980a).

Flower, L. S., and Hayes, J. R. The dynamics of composing: Making plans and juggling constraints. In L. W. Gregg and E. R. Steinberg (Eds.), *Cognitive processes in writing*. Hillsdale, N. J.: Erlbaum (1980b).

Focus: Learning to read. Focus No 4. Princeton, N. J.: Educational Testing Service (1978).

Fowler, H. W. *Dictionary of modern English usage* (2nd Edn.). Oxford University Press (1974).

Frase, L. T. Writing, text, and the reader. In C. H. Frederiksen and J. F. Dominic (Eds.), *Writing: Process, development, and communication*. Hillsdale, N. J.: Erlbaum (1981).

Frase, L. T. The UNIX Writer's Workbench software: Philosophy. *The Bell System Technical Journal*, *6*, 1883–1890 (1983).

Frederiksen, C. H. Representing logical and semantic structure of knowledge acquired from discourse. *Cognitive Psychology*, *7*, 371–458 (1975).

Frederiksen, C. H., and Dominic, J. F. (Eds.) *Writing: Process, development, and communication*. Volume 2 of *Writing: The nature, development, and teaching of written communication*. Hillsdale, N. J.: Erlbaum (1981).

Freedle, R., and Craun, M. Observations with self-embedded

sentences using written aids. *Perception and Psychophysics, 1*, 247–9 (1970).

Fry, E. B. *Teaching faster reading*. Cambridge University Press (1963).

Fry, E. B. Fry's Readability Graph: Clarifications, validity, and extension to level 17. *Journal of Reading, 21*, 242–52 (1977).

Gingrich, P. S. The UNIX Writer's Workbench software: Results of a field study. *The Bell System Technical Journal, 6*, 1909–21 (1983).

Glanzer, M., and Bowles, N. Analysis of the word-frequency effect in recognition memory. *Journal of Experimental Psychology: Human Learning and Memory, 2*, 21–31 (1976).

Goldman-Eisler, F., and Cohen, M. Is N, P, and PN difficulty a valid criterion of transformational operations? *Journal of Verbal Learning and Verbal Behavior, 9*, 161–6 (1970).

Gorman, A. M. Recognition memory for nouns as a function of abstractness and frequency. *Journal of Experimental Psychology, 61*, 23–9 (1961).

Gough, P. B. Grammatical transformations and speed of understanding. *Journal of Verbal Learning and Verbal Behavior, 4*, 107–11 (1965).

Gough, P. B. The verification of sentences: The effects of delay of evidence and sentence length. *Journal of Verbal Learning and Verbal Behavior, 5*, 492–6 (1966).

Gowers, Sir E. *The complete plain words*. (2nd Edn.) HMSO (1973).

Graves, D. H. *Writing: Teachers and children at work*. Heinemann (1983).

Graves, R., and Hodge, A. *The reader over your shoulder*. New York: Macmillan (1944).

Gregg, L. W., and Steinberg, E. R. (Eds.) *Cognitive processes in writing*. Hillsdale, N. J.: Erlbaum (1980).

Grice, H. P. Logic and conversation. In P. Cole and J. Morgan (Eds.), *Syntax and semantics III: Speech acts*. New York: Academic Press, 41–8 (1975).

Guralnik, D. B. (Ed.) *Webster's new world dictionary of the American language* (Second Coll.). New York: World Publishing Co. 1970 Edition.

Guthrie, J. T. Learnability versus readability of texts. *Journal of Educational Research*, *6*, 273–80 (1972).

Haagen, C. H. Synonymity, vividness, familiarity, and association value ratings of 400 pairs of common adjectives. *Journal of Psychology*, *27*, 453–63 (1949).

Hakes, D. T., and Cairns, H. S. Sentence comprehension and relative pronouns. *Perception and Psychophysics*, *8*, 5–8 (1970).

Halliday, M. A. K., and Hasan, R. *Cohesion in English*. Longman (1976).

Hamilton, H. W., and Deese, J. Comprehensibility and subject-verb relations in complex sentences. *Journal of Verbal Learning and Verbal Behavior*, *10*, 163–70 (1971).

Harrison, C. *Readability in the classroom*. Cambridge University Press (1980).

Hasher, L., and Chromiak, W. The processing of frequency information: An automatic mechanism? *Journal of Verbal Learning and Verbal Behavior*, *16*, 173–84 (1977).

Hayes, J. R., and Flower, L. S. Identifying the organization of writing processes. In L. W. Gregg and E. R. Steinberg (Eds.), *Cognitive processes in writing*. Hillsdale, N. J.: Erlbaum (1980a).

Hayes, J. R., and Flower, L. S. Writing as problem solving. *Visible Language*, *14*, 388–90 (1980b).

Hayes, J. R., and Flower, L. S. Uncovering cognitive processes in writing: An introduction to protocol analysis. In P. Mosenthal, L. Tamor, and S. A. Walmsley (Eds.), *Research on writing: Principles and methods*. New York: Longman (1983).

Herriott, P. The comprehension of sentences as a function of grammatical depth and order. *Journal of Verbal Learning and Verbal Behavior*, *7*, 938–41 (1968).

Hirsch, E. D. *The philosophy of composition*. Chicago: University of Chicago Press (1977).

Hobbs, J. R. Coherence and coreference. *Cognitive Science*, *3*, 67–90 (1979).

Hodges, J. C., and Whitten, M. E. *Harbrace college handbook* (Eighth Edition). New York: Harcourt, Brace, Jovanovich (1977).

Irwin, J. W. The effects of explicitness and clause order on the comprehension of reversible causal relationships. *Reading Research Quarterly*, *15*, 477–88 (1980a).

Irwin, J. W. The effects of linguistic cohesion on prose comprehension. *Journal of Reading Behaviour*, *12*, 325–32 (1980b).

Irwin, J. W. Implicit connectives and comprehension. *Reading Teacher*, *33*, 527–9 (1980c).

Irwin, J. W. The effects of coherence explicitness on college readers' prose comprehension. *Journal of Reading Behavior*, *14*, 275–84 (1982).

Irwin, J. W., and Davis, C. A. Assessing readability: The checklist approach. *Journal of Reading*, *24*, 124–30 (1980).

Kagan, J., and Havemann, E. *Psychology: An introduction* (Third Edition). New York: Harcourt, Brace, Jovanovich (1976).

Kern, R. P., Sticht, T. G., and Fox, L. C. Readability, reading ability, and readership HumRRO Professional Paper 17–70. Alexandria, Virginia: Human Resources Research Organization (1970).

Kincaid, J. P., Aagard, J. A., O'Hara, J. W., and Cottrell, L. K. Computer Readability Editing System. *IEEE Transactions on Professional Communication*, *PC 24*, No. 1, 38–41 (1981).

Kincaid, J. P., Braby, R., and Wulfeck, W. H. Computer aids for editing test questions. *Educational Technology*, June, 29–33 (1983).

Kintsch, W. *The representation of meaning in memory*. Hillsdale, N. J.: Erlbaum (1974).

Kintsch, W. On modelling comprehension. *Educational Psychologist*, *14*, 3–14 (1979).

Kintsch, W., and Keenan, J. M. Reading rate and retention as a function of the number of propositions in the base structure of sentences. *Cognitive Psychology*, *5*, 257–74 (1973).

Kintsch, W., and Vipond, D. Reading comprehension and readability, in educational practice and psychological theory. In L-G. Nilsson (Ed.), *Perspectives on memory research*. Hillsdale, N. S.: Erlbaum (1979).

Kintsch, W., and Yarbrough, J. C. Role of rhetorical structure in text comprehension. *Journal of Educational Psychology*, *74*, 828–34 (1982).

Kirkman, J. *Good style for scientific and engineering writing*. Pitman (1980).

Klare, G. R. *The measurement of readability*. Ames, Iowa: Iowa State University Press (1963).

Klare, G. R. The role of word frequency in readability. In J. R. Bormuth (Ed.), *Readability in 1968*. Champaign, Illinois: National Council of Teachers of English (1968).

Klare, G. R. Assessing readability. *Reading Research Quarterly, 10*, 62–102 (1974–75).

Klare, G. R. A second look at the validity of readability formulas. *Journal of Reading Behavior, 8*, 129–52 (1976).

Klare, G. R. Readability. In H. E. Mitzel (Ed.), *Encyclopedia of educational research* (Fifth Edition). New York: The Free Press (1982).

Klare, G. R. Readability. In P. D. Pearson (Ed.), *Handbook of reading research*. New York: Longman (1984).

Klare, G. R. Some suggestions for clear writing found in fifteen source books. Athens, Ohio: Ohio University. (Unpublished) (Undated).

Klare, G. R., and Smart, K. Analysis of the readability level of selected USAFI printed instructional materials. *Journal of Educational Research, 67*, 176 (1973).

Kniffin, J. D. The new readability requirements for military technical manuals. *Technical Communication, 26*, No. 3, 16–19 (1979).

Kniffin, J. D. Computer-aided editing – present and future. Columbia, Maryland: Westinghouse Electric Corporation. (Unpublished) (Undated).

Kucern, H., and Francis, W. N. *Computational analysis of present-day American English*. Providence, R. I.: Brown University Press (1967).

Langer, J. A. Musings. *Research in the Teaching of English, 18*, 117–18 (1984).

Lefrere, P., Macdonald-Ross, M., Waller, R., and Abbott, P. Effective forms: A Case Study of the development and testing of two Postal Claim Forms for Supplementary Benefit. The Open University (1983).

Longley, C. (Ed.) *BBC adult literacy handbook*. BBC Publications (1975).

Luzzatto, J., and Morehead, L. (Eds.) *The new American Roget's college thesaurus*. New York: The New American Library. A Signet paperback (1962).

Macdonald, N. H. The UNIX Writer's Workbench software: Rationale and design. *The Bell System Technical Journal, 6*, 1891–1908 (1983).

Macdonald, N. H., Frase, L. T., Gingrich, P. S., and Keenan, S. A. The Writer's Workbench: Computer aids for text analysis. *Educational Psychologist, 17,* 172–9 (1982).

MacGinitie, W. W., and Tretiak, R. Sentence depth measures as predictors of reading difficulty. *Reading Research Quarterly, 6,* 364–77 (1971).

Mager, R. F. *Preparing instructional objectives.* Second Edition. Belmont, California: Fearon-Pitman (1975).

Marks, L. E. Some structural and sequential factors in the processing of sentences. *Journal of Verbal Learning and Verbal Behavior, 6,* 707–13 (1967).

Marshall, N. Readability and comprehensibility. *Journal of Reading,* March, 542–4 (1979).

Marshall, N., and Glock, M. D. Comprehension of connected discourse: a style into the relationships between the structure of text and information recalled. *Reading Research Quarterly, 14,* 10–56 (1978–79).

Martin, E., and Roberts, K. H. Grammatical factors in sentence retention. *Journal of Verbal Learning and Verbal Behavior, 5,* 211–18 (1966).

Mason, G. E., Blanchard, J. S., and Daniel, D. B. *Computer applications in reading* (Second Edition). Newark, Delaware: International Reading Association (1983).

McDonald, D. A. Drafting documents in plain language. New York: Practicing Law Institute (1979).

Mehler, J. Some effects of grammatical transformation on the recall of English sentences. *Journal of Verbal Learning and Verbal Behavior, 2,* 346–51 (1963).

Meyer, B. J. F. *The organization of prose and its effects on memory.* Amsterdam: North-Holland Publishing Co (1975a).

Meyer, B. J. F. Identification of the structure of prose and its implications for the study of reading and memory. *Journal of Reading Behavior, 7,* 7–47 (1975b).

Meyer, B. J. F., and Freedle, R. The effects of different discourse types on recall. Princeton, New Jersey: Educational Testing Service (1978).

Meyer, B. J. F., and Freedle, R. Effects of discourse type on recall. *American Educational Research Journal, 21,* 121–43 (1984).

Miller, G. A. Language and psychology. In E. H. Lenneberg (Ed.), *New directions in the study of language*. Cambridge, Massachusetts: MIT Press (1964).

Miller, J. R., and Kintsch, W. Readability and recall of short prose passages: A theoretical analysis. *Journal of Experimental Psychology: Human Learning and Memory, 6*, 335–54 (1980).

Montague, W. E., and Carter, J. F. Vividness of imagery in recalling connected discourse. *Journal of Educational Psychology, 64*, 72–5 (1973).

Mosenthal, P., Tamor, L., and Walmsley, S. A. *Research on writing: Principles and methods*. New York: Longman (1983).

Mugford, L. A new way of predicting readability. *Reading, 4, 2,* 31–5 (1970).

Murphy, D. R. How plain talk increases readership 45 per cent to 66 per cent. *Printer's Ink, 220*, 35–7 (1947).

Murphy, R. Adult functional reading study. Final Report, Project No. 0-9004, PR 73-48. Princeton, New Jersey: Educational Testing Service (1973).

New plain language laws. *Simply Stated*, November, No. 31, 1, 4 (1982).

New York State Assembly. Plain English Law, introduced 18 April, 1978.

New York Times. Volunteer Army is focus of new talk about draft. 10 June 1977, p. 42 (1977).

Nystrand, M. (Ed.) *What writers know: The language, process, and structure of written discourse*. New York: Academic Press (1982).

Opdycke, J. B. *Harper's English grammar* (Revised Edition). New York: Popular Library (1977).

Paivio, A. Mental imagery in associative learning and memory. *Psychological Review, 76*, 241–63 (1969).

Paivio, A., Yuille, J. C., and Madigan, S. A. Concreteness, imagery, and meaningfulness values of 925 nouns. *Journal of Experimental Psychology, Monograph Supplement, 76*, Whole Part 2 (1968).

Palermo, D. S., and Jenkins, J. J. *Word Association norms, grade school through college*. Minneapolis: University of Minnesota Press (1964).

Partridge, E. *Usage and abusage*, New York: Hamish Hamilton (1965); Penguin (1973).

Pearson, P. D., and Camperell, K. Comprehension of text structures. In J. T. Guthrie (Ed.), *Comprehension and teaching: Research reviews*. Newark, Delaware: International Reading Association (1981).

Plain language laws – myth and reality. *Simply Stated*, December–January, No. 32, 3–4 (1982–83).

Plain language laws: Update. *Simply Stated*, February–March, No. 24, 3 (1982).

Postman, L., and Keppel, G. *Norms of word association*. New York: Academic Press (1970).

Prentice, J. Response strength of single words as an influence in sentence behavior. *Journal of Verbal Learning and Verbal Behavior*, 5, 429–33 (1966).

Pressman, R. Legislative and regulatory progress on the readability of insurance policies. Unpublished. (1979). (Available from Document Design Center, American Institutes for Research, 1055 Thomas Jefferson Street, NW, Washington, DC 20007.)

Ramsey, R. D. Grammatical voice and person in technical writing. *Journal of Technical Writing and Communication*, 10, 109–13 (1980).

Rayner, Sir Derek. Review of administrative forms. Report to the Prime Minister, Management and Personnel Office (1982).

Reder, L. M. The role of elaboration in the comprehension and retention of prose: A critical review. *Review of Educational Research*, 50, 5–53 (1980).

Redish, J. C. Readability. In D. B. Felker (Ed.) Document design: Review of the literature in six related disciplines. Washington, DC: American Institutes for Research (1980).

Richards, L. G. Concreteness as a variable in word recognition. *American Journal of Psychology*, 89, 707–18 (1976).

Richards, L. G., and Heller, F. P. Recognition thresholds as a function of word length. *American Journal of Psychology*, 89, 455–66 (1976).

Rohrman, N. L. The role of syntactic structure in the recall of English nominalizations. *Journal of Verbal Learning and Verbal Behavior*, 7, 904–12 (1968).

Rosenberg, S. Recall of sentences as a function of syntactic and associative habit. *Journal of Verbal Learning and Verbal Behavior*, 5, 392–6 (1966).

Rothkopf, E. Ten years of prose learning research. Invited address, Division C, American Educational Research Association, New York (1977).

Russell, B. How I write. In R. E. Egner and L. E. Denonn (Eds.), *The basic writings of Bertrand Russell, 1903–1959*. George Allen and Unwin, Ltd. (1961).

Samuels, S. J. Effect of word associations on reading speed, recall, and guessing behavior on tests. *Journal of Educational Psychology, 59,* 12–15 (1968).

Savin, H. B., and Perchonock, E. Grammatical structure and the immediate recall of English sentences. *Journal of Verbal Learning and Verbal Behavior, 4,* 348–53 (1965).

Schlesinger, I. M. *Sentence structure and the reading process.* The Hague: Mouton (1968).

Schumacher, G. M., Klare, G. R., Cronin, F. C., and Moses, J. D. Cognitive activities of beginning and advanced college writers: A pausal analysis. *Research in the Teaching of English, 18,* 169–87 (1984).

Schuyler, M. R. A readability program for use on microcomputers. *Journal of Reading, 25,* 560–91 (1982).

Sheffield, A. D. (Ed.) *Soule's dictionary of English synonyms.* Boston: Little, Brown and Co. A Bantam paperback (1959).

Shimmerlik, S. M. Organization theory and memory for prose: A review of the literature. *Review of Educational Research, 48,* 103–20 (1978).

Slobin, D. I. Grammatical transformations and sentence comprehension in childhood and adulthood. *Journal of Verbal Learning and Verbal Behavior, 5,* 219–27 (1966).

Slobin, D. I. Recall of full and truncated passive sentences in connected discourse. *Journal of Verbal Learning and Verbal Behavior, 7,* 876–81 (1968).

Smith, F. *Understanding reading* (third Edition). New York: Holt, Rinehart, and Winston (1982).

Spreen, O., and Schulz, R. W. Parameters of abstraction, meaningfulness, and pronunciability for 329 nouns. *Journal of Verbal Learning and Verbal Behavior, 5,* 459–68 (1966).

Sticht, T. G. Research towards the design, development, and evaluation of a job-functional literacy program for the US Army. *Literacy Discussion IV, 3,* September, 339–69 (1973).

Sticht, T. G., Kern, R. P., Caylor, J. S., and Fox, L. C.

Determining literacy requirements of jobs: Progress and prospects for Project REALISTIC HumRRO Professional Paper 13–70. Alexandria, Virginia: Human Resources Research Organization (1970).

Stoodt, B. D. The relationship between understanding grammatical conjunctions and reading comprehension. *Elementary English*, 49, 513–16 (1972).

Strunk, W., and White, E. B. *The elements of style* (Third Edition). New York: The Macmillan Co (1979).

Swanson, C. E. Readability and readership: A controlled experiment. *Journalism Quarterly*, 25, 339–43 (1948).

Thorndike, E. L. Reading as reasoning: A study of mistakes in paragraph reading. *The Journal of Educational Psychology*, 8, 323–32 (1917).

Thorndike-Barnhart handy dictionary. Garden City, New York: Doubleday and Co., Inc. (1944). A Bantam paperback (1955).

Thorndike, E. L., and Lorge, I. *The teacher's word book of 30 000 words*. New York: Bureau of Publications, Teachers College, Columbia University (1944).

Thorndike, R. L., and Garrettson, E. What makes a word difficult? Teachers College, Columbia, University. (Unpublished) (1968).

Toglia, M. P., and Battig, W. F. *Handbook of semantic word norms*. Hillsdale, New Jersey: Erlbaum (1978).

United Kingdom. Administrative forms in government. Cmnd. 8504. Her Majesty's Stationery Office (1982).

US Navy. Solicitation No. N66001-79-R-0403. Issued by Supply Officer, Naval Ocean Systems Center (San Diego, California) (1979).

van Dijk, T. A. Macro-structures, knowledge frames and discourse comprehension. In M. A. Just and P. Carpenter (Eds.), *Cognitive processes in comprehension*. Hillsdale, N. J.: Erlbaum (1977).

Walker, H. J. Imagery ratings for 338 nouns. *Behavior Research Methods and Instrumentation*, 2, 165–7 (1970).

Waller, R. Designing a government form: A case study. *Information Design Journal*, 4, 36–57 (1984).

Wang, M. D. The role of syntactic complexity as a determiner of comprehensibility. *Journal of Verbal Learning and Verbal Behavior*, *9*, 398–404 (1970).

Wearing, A. J. Remembering complex sentences. *Quarterly Journal of Experimental Psychology*, *24*, 77–86 (1972).

West, M. *The new method English dictionary explaining the meaning of 24,000 items within a vocabulary of 1,490 words*. Longmans, Green (1935).

West, M. *A general service list of English words*. New York: Longmans (1953).

Yngve, V. H. A model and an hypothesis for language structure. *Proceedings of the American Philosophical Society*, *104*, 444–6 (1960).

Young, P. T. *Motivation and emotions: A survey of the determiners of human and animal activity*. New York: Wiley (1961).

Yuille, J. C., and Paivio, A. Abstractness and the recall of connected discourse. *Journal of Educational Psychology*, *82*, 467–71 (1969).

Zipf, G. K. *Human behavior and the principle of least effort*. Cambridge, Massachusetts: Addison-Wesley (1949).

Name Index

Aagard, J. A., 79
Abbott, P., 24
Anderson, P. V., 78
Anderson, R. C., 40, 46, 68
Atlas, M. A., 39, 58

Bach, Emmon, 101
Barnhart, C. L., 88
Bastian, J., 91
Battig, William, 89, 93
Bendick, M., 21
Berkeley, Edmund, 31
Blanchard, J. S., 116
Blount, H. P., 99
Blumenfeld, P. J., 91
Blumenthal, A. L., 99
Bormuth, J. R., 90, 92, 99
Bowles, N., 90
Braby, R., 79
Bransford, John, 68
Britton, B. K., 70
Britton, J., 78
Brockman, R. J., 78
Burgess, T., 78

Cairns, H. S., 99
Calkins, L. M., 78

Camperell, K., 69, 84
Cantu, M. G., 21
Carpenter, P. A., 35
Carroll, John, 40, 42, 88
Carter, J. F., 91
Carter, Jimmy, 23
Chall, Jeanne, 113
Chromiak, W., 87
Churchill, Winston, 86
Cliff, Norman, 94
Cohen, Michele, 104
Coleman, E. B., 90, 91, 92, 98, 99
Cottrell, L. K., 79
Cronin, Frank, 61, 71, 78

Dale, Edgar, 93, 113
Daniel, D. B., 116
Davies, P., 88
Davis, C. A., 112
Deese, J., 99
Dominic, J. F., 78
Duffy, Thomas, 22
Dukes, W. F., 91

Elley, W. B., 90, 91
Ellis, H. C., 43
Emig, Janet, 78

Topic Index